HIDDEN HISTORY
of
BURNET COUNTY

Suzanne Warwick Freeman

THE
History
PRESS

Published by The History Press
An imprint of Arcadia Publishing
Charleston, SC
www.historypress.com

First published 2025

Manufactured in the United States

ISBN 9781467158862

Library of Congress Control Number: 2024950544

Notice: The information in this book is true and complete to the best of our knowledge. It is offered without guarantee on the part of the author or The History Press. The author and The History Press disclaim all liability in connection with the use of this book.

Dedicated to my mother, Frances Naomi Clark, who died on June 13, 2023, and my amazing aunt, Mary Elizabeth Clark Wimberly, both of whom grew up in a house made of stone in the shadow of Granite Mountain and the Old Granite School in Marble Falls, where they learned to read.

CONTENTS

ACKNOWLEDGEMENTS

Much of the history recorded in this collection has been told many times in many formats. My goal has been to expand the research, connect the past to the present and tell the story of a community through the eyes of the people who built it. I've relied on archives, old news articles and stories from the descendants of founding families.

This is not an endeavor done alone or without dedication and passion from a variety of players. This collection could not have been written without the help of people like Robyn Richter, who dug through files and answered dozens of phone calls, emails and texts to help fill in the blanks for several of these stories. Her roots run deep in Hill Country history, starting with her German immigrant ancestors. She has turned her connection with Texas history into a commitment to the community. As she conducts her own personal family research, she also donates her time and resources to the Falls on the Colorado Museum board of directors, where she is a member and has served as chairman. She's not the only board member who deserves my gratitude.

Former chairman and current board member Darlene Oostermeyer has had her fingers in just about every history-based research project I have ever embarked on ever. We share a family duty as members of the Richland Cemetery Association and a love for the Old Granite School that houses the museum. That building was where my maternal grandmother, mother, aunt and uncle all received parts of their education and where Darlene visited in the summer to slide down the old fire escape. Both of our roots are deep in Burnet County.

Another former chairman, Amanda Seim, pulled files, sat for interviews and answered nitpicky questions with a smile no matter how often I called. She wears multiple local history hats. In addition to her volunteer positions on the Burnet County Historical Commission (BCHC) and the Falls Museum board, she is the genealogy librarian at the Herman Brown Free Library in Burnet.

That amazing library maintains a deep, rich and rewarding archive under the leadership of library director Florence Reeves. It's also a great place to hang out and work. Thanks for providing a second work home, Florence!

Debbie Holloway deserves acknowledgment from me for helping with research and contacts, but also from the entire Highland Lakes community for Legends of the Falls, a theatrical hayride through history that got bigger and better each of its three years (2021–23). Holloway continues to feed interest in local history with an active Legends of the Falls Facebook page.

Another rich store of information also came through the Burnet County Historical Commission, which recently moved into the Old Burnet County Jail. Many of the people who serve on that county board live on the family ranches where they grew up. Their files, their connections and their memories were priceless in helping me write this book.

Special thanks go to Rachel Bryson, Lela Goar and Tommye Dorbandt Potts, all doyennes of community, culture and class. If they don't know the answers to my questions, they know who does. Each of them has gone out of her way to make sure I got the information, got it right and got it on time.

Ann Nelson and Paula Hesse at the Fort Croghan Museum and Grounds have left the comfort of their homes many times to open up the building and its archives for my inquiries, even during off hours.

I also want to thank Dr. Jane Knapik, a trained historian and retired teacher who is a member of both the Falls on the Colorado Museum board and the BCHC. She is also coauthor with Marble Falls librarian Amanda Rose of *Images of America: Marble Falls*, published by Arcadia Publishing, August 2013, one of several books that inspired this one.

And thanks to Bob Kent, a much more tenacious historian than I will ever be. When I find a hole in my research, he usually has just what I need to fill in the blanks.

While all these people helped with information and images, two people at my workplace, Victory Media in Marble Falls, made sure my words and the images were as close to perfect as possible. Creative Director David Bean scanned and photographed many of the pictures in this book. He also took the author photo, which proves he can work miracles with a tough subject.

Managing Editor Wendi Wilkerson used her amazing wordsmith skills to correct my missteps along the way. She read all but two of these stories long before they were slated for this publication.

Special thanks go to my employer, Victory Media, where I have been executive editor for the last twelve years, although my connection to the company and the family that founded it goes back much further. Victory Media publishes *The Picayune Magazine*, among other titles, where many of these stories first appeared. Owner Amber Weems gave enthusiastic permission to repackage and republish when the project was presented to her. All the stories have been updated and, in some cases, reworked or combined for this collection.

I hope you enjoy reading them as much as I enjoyed researching and writing them. There are many more where these came from.

PREFACE

These stories are a collection of articles first published in some form in *The Picayune Magazine*, a monthly magazine that covers the people and places of Burnet and Llano Counties. I have combined some, updated others and, in all cases, improved the writing. My motto: no story is ever really finished, especially history!

The Picayune was a weekly newspaper in the Highland Lakes in Central Texas for twenty-seven years. I took over as executive editor in 2018, when it was converted to a monthly magazine. One of the many joys I have experienced working with Victory Media, publisher of *The Picayune, 101 Fun Things to Do in the Highland Lakes* and DailyTrib.com, is having the luxury of researching and writing about the area's rich history. *The Picayune Magazine* continues to be an amazing platform for preserving that history.

PART I

———•———

BUILT UPON THIS ROCK

Chapter 1

SISTERS OF STONE IN SUNSET RED

More than 1.1 billion years ago, two magma chambers broke through the crust of the earth at nearly the same time and depth some sixty miles apart in Central Texas. Through several geologic processes loosely termed the Llano uplift, they were exposed at the surface and are now known as Granite Mountain in Marble Falls and Enchanted Rock between Llano and Fredericksburg. And while the largest of the pair is called a rock and the smallest a mountain, technically, they are neither. According to geology experts, the two granite formations are individual plutons formed separately from the same batholith, a massive formation of igneous rock deep in the earth. The Enchanted Rock batholith stretches at least sixty-two miles underground.

Sisters in formation and mineralogy, their lives have taken very different turns in the last 150 years—a minuscule blip on their granitic timelines. They stand as direct opposites in terms of how each has been defined and used as a valuable resource by their communities.

GRANITE MOUNTAIN

Once the largest employer in Marble Falls, Granite Mountain has shrunk in workforce and size over the years as its Texas sunset red granite was blasted, cut and shipped around the globe for monuments, state buildings,

Granite Mountain, pictured here in the mid-1880s, has been a quarry for 137 years. It is connected underground to Enchanted Rock, some sixty miles away. *Falls on the Colorado Museum.*

skyscrapers and jetties. For the last 137 years, men have quarried it for profit, a decision that has helped shape the city and the state.

"The biggest thing is that it put Marble Falls on the map just because of the capitol and the history," said John Packer, who worked at the mountain for sixteen years, ten as general manager. He is the owner of Alexis Granite and a former mayor of Marble Falls. "It has a huge connection to the capitol and state history, and that will be here forever."

At its peak, the mountain employed around five hundred people, including when some three hundred convicts carved out the stone that built the state capitol in Austin in the 1880s. Only about sixty employees work there now.

"There are very few people raised here in the 1960s and '70s who didn't either work there or have someone close to them work there," said Mike Clark, who spent thirty years at Texas Granite. His father, James Clark,

who worked for Texas Granite for eighteen years, was killed in an industrial accident at the Texas Pearl quarry in Granite Shoals in 1973. Mike was fourteen. Despite the tragedy, Mike went to work at Granite Mountain four years later—against his mother's wishes.

"I was fresh out of high school, and Mom really didn't want me to, but he would have wanted me to," Clark said, referring to his father. "I wanted to go to work. That mountain fed me when I was a kid, and it fed my family. It helped me raise my family."

Another longtime employee, Joe Walker, worked the quarry for twenty-five years. Like Clark, he started full-time after graduation. During his middle and high school years, he worked summer jobs there. His father and grandfather both worked the mountain. Like Packer, he now has his own granite business: Walker's Artistic Granite.

"Granite Mountain was good to my family," Walker said. "It fed a lot of people in this town. And it was something to be proud of. We were sending granite all over the world. It was a great learning experience."

First under the control of the Comanches, Granite Mountain came under Anglo ownership when the Republic of Texas granted William Slaughter a league and a labor of land totaling 4,500.5 acres. The grant included 180 acres of solid rock, which Slaughter never saw. He was given the land for agreeing to settle in Texas, but the Mississippi native never came any farther into the state than Sabine County in East Texas.

William sold his grant within two years to one of his sons, George Webb Slaughter, for $1,500. George Webb never saw the property either. A Texas hero, George fought in the war against Mexico and is known for delivering a message to Colonel William B. Travis from the commander in chief of the Texas Army, Sam Houston, to retreat from the Alamo—a message Travis ignored.

The only family member to make his home on the grant was William Ransom Slaughter, one of George Webb's eleven children. He bought up all the pieces of the original tract owned by other relatives and built a cabin there for him and his wife to start a family. She died soon after they settled.

William Ransom brought a second wife to Burnet County and sold the eastern half of the original grant in 1882 to George W. Lacy for $3,453. In brokering a deal for the grassland around the rock, Lacy told Slaughter he wouldn't give more than a "packsaddle and the mule I'm leading" for the 180-acre mountain. Slaughter didn't want to be left with a giant rock he would have to pay taxes on, so he made the exchange.

Lacy was the first owner of the giant granite outcropping who saw it as a way to make a living. After he purchased the property, he sold a one-third interest to N.L. Norton and one-third to W.H. Westfall to form a partnership and start a quarry.

They kicked off their business by brokering a deal with Texas Governor John Ireland to provide the Sunset Red stone for the new Texas State Capitol Building in exchange for a railroad spur from Fairland to Marble Falls to the mountain—a total of six miles. The state also agreed to provide 300 convicts to work the quarry for sixty-five cents per ten-hour day. The money was paid to the superintendent of prisons. As part of the agreement, Lacy's company provided room and board for the convicts, who worked alongside 148 paid stonecutters. Those 448 men cut fifty thousand tons of rock from the mountain, which were shipped in 15,700 cars to Austin. Blocks of granite that fell off the train cars can still be found along the tracks.

In 1890, after the capitol was complete, the three men formed the Texas Capitol Granite Company, valued at $200,000. They sold it in 1903 to Robert Caterson and Thomas Darragh of New York, who in turn formed the Texas and New York Granite Company. One version of the story set the price at $100,000; another version said it sold for $1 million. In 1926, Caterson sold his half to Robert Clark, and the name changed to Texas Pink Granite Company. Darragh and Clark abandoned the quarry in 1929, the year the Great Depression began.

In 1951, the mountain changed hands again, this time selling to its current owners, Cold Spring Granite of Cold Spring, Minnesota. A family-owned company, Cold Spring has seven different quarries in the Highland Lakes, making a total of thirty around the country. Each of the quarries produces a different color of granite.

During its peak years through the early 1990s, Granite Mountain produced the stone for some of the most iconic buildings in the world, including what is now the Sears Tower in Chicago; the Coca-Cola Building in Atlanta; and the Grand Central Station office building, the Whitney Museum and the East Wing of the Museum of Natural History in New York. Sunset Red has been used in skyscrapers in Australia, Thailand and other countries. Most state buildings in Austin are built of Sunset Red, as are many of the county courthouses, including the Bexar County Courthouse in San Antonio.

Changes in technology and building materials have led to a decrease in the need for granite. Many of the iconic buildings of the past used three-inch-thick slabs. Now, only about an inch is needed for the same durability and strength. Also, Cold Spring no longer processes the granite in Marble Falls. The giant blocks are shipped to Minnesota to be cut and polished and then shipped again to the customer. The cost of transportation has priced the stone out of the market for locals wanting a piece of polished Sunset Red in their homes.

The old mountain may still have some life left in it, according to Packer.

"The market is cyclical," he said. "With architects, you go through phases of nothing but granite, then all of a sudden everything is glass. It all depends on the market and design. Granite's still popular; it's just in a down cycle."

All three former employees talk of the pride they feel having worked on some of the bigger projects and seeing some of the mountain's history firsthand.

"As little kids, we used to climb all over that mountain," Walker said. "Where the cave is, out there by itself, there's a lot of artifacts up there around the rocks from when they had prisoners in there."

Enchanted Rock

As Granite Mountain is closed to the public—and dwindling away—the best place to see what the mountain looked like before companies began moving it around the world piece by piece is at Enchanted Rock, which experienced a much different history in the last century and a half.

During peak seasons, the line of cars waiting to enter Enchanted Rock State Natural Area can stretch for two miles or more. Park Superintendent Doug Cochran attributes it to the allure of climbing the 425-foot summit of the park's central feature, a pink granite dome that covers 640 acres of the Texas Hill Country, and the great camping and hiking available.

Enchanted Rock became a designated National Natural Landmark in 1971 and was added to the U.S. National Register of Historic Places on August 29, 1984. In 2017, the park was rated the best campsite in Texas in a fifty-state survey conducted by MSN.com. Today, it draws 300,000 visitors annually and can have as many as 3,000 in one weekend.

"There is an economic impact on surrounding communities from Enchanted Rock," Cochran said of the park's popularity.

For many fans of the park, it's more than a great place to camp. Llano resident Ira Kennedy, who published *Enchanted Rock Magazine* from 1993

Enchanted Rock, in a state park near Llano, is connected underground to Granite Mountain, a quarry in Marble Falls. *The Picayune Magazine.*

to 1998, spoke reverently of the spiritual nature of the granite batholith. He tells of a live oak tree that grew on the summit until it was struck by lightning, comparing it to the Tree of Life in the Book of Genesis—not such a stretch considering the age of the rock and the spiritual impact it has had for so many over the centuries.

"That image grabs you and puts you into the realm of the mythical," Kennedy said. "You're going to take something spiritual from there. It will have an effect."

When Kennedy visits Enchanted Rock, also a frequent subject of his art, he goes to connect to nature and for the sense of peace that seems to radiate from the trails and granite outcroppings that surround the dome.

"People go up there for ceremony and ritual," Kennedy said. "And others, if you will, go up to 'get well again.' They go to recharge their spiritual as well as their emotional batteries. That's what it does for you."

Located off Texas 16 between Fredericksburg and Llano, Enchanted Rock remains almost exactly as it was when humans first encountered it. Geologists date it at about 1.1 billion years old, the largest pink granite pluton in the United States.

The rock almost met the same fate as Granite Mountain. Straddling the Llano and Gillespie County line, the bigger rock and the land around it changed hands many times before becoming a campground and eventually a state natural area.

Until the mid-1800s, the only human inhabitants were Native Americans. Flint-tipped spears, arrowheads and other artifacts dating to eleven thousand years ago turn up after heavy rains. The rock's fate, untouched for millions of years, became uncertain once it became a deeded piece of property that could change hands.

Sam Maverick was one of the first known owners. A legendary Texas investor, land baron and cattleman, Samuel Augustus Maverick was one of the signers of the Texas Declaration of Independence. A man who refused to brand his cattle, his name came to stand for anyone with an independent spirit. He settled in San Antonio with his family in the late 1800s and owned both the property and mineral rights to Enchanted Rock.

After Maverick died in 1870, his widow sold the property to N.P.P. Browne. In 1886, John R. Moss bought it and then gave ownership to C.T. Moss, J.D. Slaytor and A.F. Moss a year later.

"Enchanted Rock traded hands amongst the Moss family like a game of musical chairs," said Kennedy, who has conducted extensive research on the property.

That is, until it ended up with Charles Moss, who opened the area to the public for social gatherings and camping. In 1978, he offered it to the Texas Parks and Wildlife Department (TPWD) for $1.3 million. TPWD turned him down—at first.

Once word spread that Enchanted Rock was for sale, the Moss family received all sorts of offers from quarries and developers. One Dallas developer wanted to build townhomes there. Perhaps the most intriguing suggestion came from Lincoln Borglum, the son of Gutzon Borglum, who designed Mount Rushmore. Lincoln wanted to sculpt a monument in honor of Texas heroes on the face of the rock.

Then a former first lady with ties to the Hill Country heard about the plans. "Lady Bird Johnson saw what was going to happen," Cochran said. "She got the powers at Texas Parks and Wildlife, the National Park Service and the Nature Conservancy on board."

The Nature Conservancy bought Enchanted Rock while the state organized funds. A month later, the conservancy sold it to TPWD. The park is still growing. In the fall of 2024, TPWD announced the purchase of an adjacent 600 acres to expand the park by around one-third. The park will expand from 1,650 acres to 2,280 acres.

While Cochran credits Johnson for saving Enchanted Rock, Kennedy also cites the Moss family for holding onto the property for so long without altering it.

"The Moss family deserves credit for protecting this place," Kennedy said. "We could be sitting among condos."

With fierce competition among other parks and reserves for state funding, fans of the Rock established a nonprofit organization, the Friends of Enchanted Rock, to pay for park needs not covered in the state budget. The Friends host an annual rock climbing competition, the Granite Gripper, which is one of the oldest climbing competitions in the United States.

The Rock regularly hosts rock climbing events, including for groups like the Boy Scouts and Girls Scouts, who come to earn badges in a variety of outdoor activities.

"Enchanted Rock has endured in its present form for eons," Kennedy said. "The marginal changes that have been made since the park opened haven't really affected Enchanted Rock itself. It was here before humans, and it will be here long after we leave."

Chapter 2

THE TOWN BUILT BY A BLIND MAN

The vision of a blind man carved the community of Marble Falls from the limestone and granite that eventually put it on the economic map of a burgeoning new state. Adam Rankin Johnson could see perfectly well in 1854 when he first laid eyes on the bucolic hills surrounding the Colorado River as it snaked its way through the Texas Hill Country. He was working as a surveyor at the time, making note of much more than the coordinates of a plat as he took in the topography and rich resources available.

Called to fight for the Confederacy, Rankin returned from the Civil War as a general in 1865, a former prisoner of war who had been blinded by friendly fire. His loss of sight did not affect the Kentucky native's ability to see a bright future for his adopted homeland.

Johnson could hear the sound of success in the roaring falls for which the town was eventually named. In that crash of water on rock, he heard the potential to generate electricity and industry. With the help of his son and two newly freed Black residents who served as his eyes and carriage drivers, Johnson began laying out city streets on a numbered grid, counting from the river north, all based on his memory of the landscape.

Although the area mapped was named Marble Falls, the river water did not flow over marble. The limestone riverbed glittered like marble when wet, leading to its incorrect moniker. Many people, however, called the area the "Blind Man's Town." Fortunately, the name Marble Falls is the one that stuck.

General Adam R. Johnson stands next to the Marble Falls town cornerstone, which is now on the grounds of the Falls on the Colorado Museum. *Falls on the Colorado Museum.*

FLAMES OF FORTUNE

Marble Falls got its first lucky break from tragedy: a fire that destroyed the original state capitol building in Austin in 1881. Texas Governor John Ireland wanted to build a new structure from limestone, but Marble Falls locals George Lacy, Dr. W.H. Westfall and N.L. Norton lobbied for a much more durable material.

The three men owned Granite Mountain northwest of the city's center. They traded Texas legislators free granite for a railway spur from Burnet, which literally put Marble Falls on the map. A decision to use cheap convict labor to mine the granite created waves of controversy that eventually washed up on the shores of Scotland. When the motherland sent skilled stonecutters to help the untrained convicts, union leaders tried to physically stop them as they stepped off ships in New York and Galveston. They came on anyway.

Johnson used the impetus of the granite mining operation to form the Texas Mining and Improvement Company (TM&I). The official birthday of the city of Marble Falls is based on the creation of that entity, which occurred on July 6, 1887. Within a week, Johnson held a public sales event on a grandstand in the center of town. Some three thousand people showed up to buy lots, which sold from $75 to $750.

As tracks were laid for the railroad spur, George and Elizabeth Roper built the Roper Hotel, which still stands at 707 Third Street on U.S. Highway 281. It now houses several businesses and was once a restaurant.

The train came in 1889, followed by a depot, which became the center of town activity. The depot was moved in 1976 to the city's new center of town, the intersection of U.S. 281 and RR 1431. It first served as a visitors' center and then an art gallery. It is now home to the Capital Area Rural Transportation System, which leases it from the city.

TM&I established the Ice, Light, and Water Company. The concrete bones of that facility can still be seen on the north shore of Lake Marble Falls, just below and west of the U.S. 281 bridge. The building was completed in 1893, powering the city and an adjacent textile plant, part of Johnson's original vision for the area. He planned to make Marble Falls the economic center of a thriving cotton and textile industry.

An iron and wood toll bridge supplemented ferry traffic to move people and supplies across the river along what is now the city's main thoroughfare, U.S. 281. A public protest against tolls led Burnet County officials to purchase the bridge and allow free public access.

Families looking to farm, ranch or own a business that catered to agriculture began to move in around the turn of the century. Johnson sold land to build a school, the Marble Falls Alliance University. That building, too, still stands.

Thousands of Marble Falls residents were educated in the Old Granite School. It became home to the newly formed Marble Falls Independent School District in 1908. It was converted to house the district's administrative offices in 1982, but students still attended classes there until 1986. It is the home of the Falls on the Colorado Museum.

Businesses have come and gone, but some, like the Blue Bonnet Cafe (named for blue hats, not the flower), remain. The Blue Bonnet has been serving its traditional country cooking since 1929. Fast-food restaurants have joined in the task of feeding the many residents, vacationers and shoppers who converge on the city year-round. With the addition of Walmart, Home Depot, Lowes, Ross and an expanded H-E-B grocery store, the city has become the region's shopping mecca.

The U.S. 281 bridge also marks the passing of time. After floods swept away the old iron and wood bridge in 1935, the Texas Department of

Transportation replaced it with a two-lane concrete and steel bridge the next year. That was widened to four lanes in 1973, and that version was blown up in 2013 to make way for its replacement.

As the city continues to grow, the old granite mountain continues to be shipped out in pieces as construction material for everything from jetties to skyscrapers. Not to worry: geologists say it will take another nine hundred years to completely deplete that resource.

Johnson's vision for the city may not have been spot on, but the area has grown in population and popularity, with a rich history driven by his foresight. At 130-plus years, the city is still young, the buildings and dams that formed it a mere speck on land with some of the oldest exposed rock in the state. Geologists estimate that Marble Falls is close to 1.36 billion years old. Now that's history.

HISTORIC HIGHLIGHTS

As the town's population grew from around 300 at the turn of the twentieth century to 8,395 as of December 2024, the city obviously went through some changes. Historic highlights include:

- installing the first telephone in 1893;
- electing Ophelia "Birdie" Crosby Harwood the nation's first woman mayor in 1917, three years before women could even vote;
- the controversial cutting down in 1924 of one-hundred-year-old oak trees that shaded the center of Main Street;
- paving streets for the first time in 1936;
- building the smallest of the six Colorado River dams, Max Starcke, which created Lake Marble Falls in 1949–51;
- naming streets and putting up the first street signs in 1956;
- moving PO box addresses to street addresses and home mail delivery in 1971.

Chapter 3

ROSA, THE FRIENDLY GHOST
IN GRANITE

If Rosa Darragh's ghost haunts the pink granite house at 501 Main Street in Marble Falls, she is a friendly ghost, according to owner Kim Lookabaugh, who opened My Texas Home Broker in the historic residence in 2020.

"We think Ms. Rosa might still be here," Lookabaugh said. "Every time something weird happens—something falls down off a shelf or there's a weird noise we can't explain—we definitely say, 'That must be Ms. Rosa.'"

The house was built for Rosa in 1935 after her husband, Thomas Darragh Jr., died that same year. A co-owner of Granite Mountain, Thomas lived with Rosa in a large two-story house at the quarry. After their father's death, Rosa's children wanted her in town so she wouldn't have to drive so far every day to a dry goods store she owned and operated.

"It was on the west side of Main Street where the flower shop is now," said Ann Darragh of Marble Falls. "I think it was called Darragh's Dry Goods."

Ann is married to Rosa and Thomas's grandson, Bob Darragh. She was referring to Marble Falls Flower and Gift Shop at 214 Main Street between Second and Third.

A New Yorker, Thomas Darragh Jr. bought the mountain in partnership with Robert Caterson in 1903. Darragh moved to Marble Falls to run the quarry, which the co-owners named the Texas and New York Granite Company. Caterson soon sold his half to Robert Clark, and the name changed to Texas Pink Granite Co.

Left: Rosa Darragh stands on the front steps of her granite home in Marble Falls on a Mother's Day in the 1950s. *Falls on the Colorado Museum.*

Below: The rock used to build 501 Main Street in Marble Falls came from rubble obtained free from Granite Mountain. *Suzanne Freeman.*

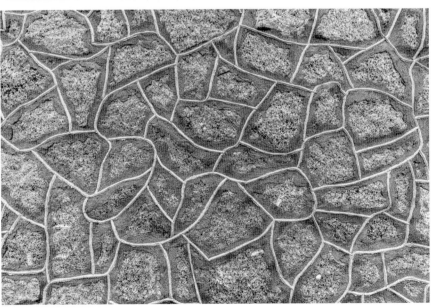

Rosa's pink granite house was built on a hill facing the mountain, which can be seen easily from the home's large stone front porch. Even the steps up to the front door are made of granite, cut from the same batholith quarried by convicts to build the state capitol in Austin.

Unlike the large blocks of stone used to construct the statehouse, the rock used to build 501 Main Street came from rubble obtained free from the mountain. Quarry managers heaped chunks of broken granite into a pile for anyone who could haul it away.

Many homes in Marble Falls were built from free granite scrap, but only Rosa's included a basement, unusual in an area with such rocky terrain. The basement has its own entrance on the south side of the house.

"When the dams were being built on the Colorado, [Rosa] sometimes moved into the basement of the house and rented out apartments or rooms to the workers," reads the caption for a picture of Rosa Darragh that is on page 81 of *Images of America: Marble Falls*, by Jane Knapik and Amanda Rose.

A solidly built home, even the inside walls are rock. Instead of drywall, the interior walls and ceiling are all mortar. The rooms are large, with ten-foot ceilings. All of the original wood floors are intact throughout the house.

Another surprise can be found in the kitchen. "It still has the original kitchen," Lookabaugh pointed out when giving a tour of the space. "And there's an iron hitching post outside for tying up your horse."

The countertop along one kitchen wall was installed in 1940. The counters are made of small white ceramic tiles. The backsplash is done in larger, dazzling green tiles. The cabinets are painted white, with retro black iron hardware.

Of course, all the plumbing and wiring were replaced years ago. Lookabaugh had to upgrade from that even to turn the residential property into a commercial enterprise. That transformation took some imagination—and drilling—when it came to lighting since wires could not be run through solid rock and mortar walls.

The sturdy materials used posed no need for extra insulation. "The energy efficiency is very good," Lookabaugh said. "It's well insulated with solid rock. There's no other insulation."

The bedrooms were turned into offices, and an old closet became a workroom. Knocking out closet space resulted in a funny little hallway area that connects a side room to a front room in a short zigzag—another creative quirk that separates it from most other houses in town, not to mention its very own ghost.

When asked about stories of a ghost, Ann and Bob Darragh said they had never heard anything like that mentioned before.

"I wouldn't be surprised though," Bob said with a laugh.

Lookabaugh likes to think Ms. Rosa is indeed sharing the house with her and her business.

"She's certainly not a scary ghost," Lookabaugh said. "This house has the best feeling. People who walk in here just love it."

As for Ms. Rosa (September 7, 1871–September 6, 1965), she is buried in the Marble Falls City Cemetery next to her husband (1867–1935). Her grave is marked with the same Texas pink granite that made her living and built her home.

PART II

SETTLERS
AND OTHER FIRSTS

Chapter 1

HISTORY UP IN FLAMES

History-loving hearts in the Highland Lakes broke as word spread that the 150-year-old Conrad Fuchs home had burned on Sunday, February 25, 2024. Crumbling rock walls are all that's left of the historic pioneer homestead in Horseshoe Bay after decades of failed attempts to preserve it as a community landmark.

"We tried everything we could to save it for the community," said Caryl Calsyn, her voice cracking when she spoke at the March 5, 2024, meeting of the Burnet County Historical Commission as members began to deal with the loss. "We cared for that house."

Calsyn is on the commission and was an active member of the Friends of the Conrad Fuchs Committee, a group that worked for years to raise restoration money and keep the house open to the community. The group was unable to raise enough money, and the property ended up in private hands, although the new owners planned to restore the house and provide public access to the property.

For a forty-year period spanning the turn of the twentieth century, much of the acreage that is now Cottonwood Shores and Horseshoe Bay South was "the hub of pioneer industry," according to the late historian Esther Richter Weaver.* The Conrad Fuchs house was called "one of the first substantial homes of a cultured pioneer family" by Weaver in her successful 1974 application to the Texas Historical Commission for a historical marker.

"[The house] is an example of what highly skilled craftsmen could accomplish during pioneer days with the natural resources at hand," Weaver wrote. "[It is] a monument to the courage and strength of the pioneers… who labored constantly against many odds in the primitive wilderness."

As renovations were underway, the historic 150-year-old Conrad Fuchs house in Horseshoe Bay burned on February 25, 2024. *The Picayune Magazine.*

Conrad Fuchs was born in Germany, the fourth child of Adolph and Luise (Rumker) Fuchs, who moved to the United States with seven of their children in 1845. Adolph and Luise were given a league of Central Texas land (around 4,400 acres) that was granted posthumously to German immigrant Ferdinand Lueders by then–Texas President Sam Houston. Lueders died from wounds sustained in the Battle of San Jacinto, fighting for Texas independence from Mexico.

Lueders's brother, a town mayor in Germany, inherited the land but had no desire to leave his native country. He gave the acreage to his good friend Reverend Adolph Fuchs. A Lutheran minister, Fuchs was looking for religious freedom and new opportunities for his large family. Adolph brought one of the first pianos to the Southwest and taught music lessons for both piano and violin.

By the way, the German pronunciation of *Fuchs* rhymes with *books*. Somewhere around the turn of the century, the name was Americanized to rhyme with *fox*. Eventually, it became Fox, a name still prevalent in Central Texas.

Although several members of the first Fuchs family stayed in the area and built homes, two of which are still standing, this story is about Conrad, his wife, Anna Perlitz, and the house they built near the Colorado River before Marble Falls was founded.

The couple married in 1860 and one year later purchased 160 acres of land adjacent to Adolph's property for eighty dollars in Confederate money. They started what became a large family in a log cabin until the two-story stone structure was completed in 1880. Conrad built the house using nearby stone for the outer walls, oak and cedar trees for the interior framing and cabinetry and even locally quarried and processed lime for mortar and plaster.

Conrad was the first postmaster of the Tiger Mill Post Office, which moved to Marble Falls when that city was founded in 1887. Pony Express riders delivering the mail and stagecoach drivers with passengers and packages pulled into a stable built under the back of the house, which extended over a rocky incline. Also on his land, Conrad built and operated a gristmill, a blacksmith shop, a cotton gin press, a sugar cane press, a sawmill and a limekiln.

Anna taught school in the area for about fifteen years, first in the log cabin and later in the stone house. She had up to fourteen students at a time, all related to the Fuchs family in some way.

The house was large and impressive, especially for such a rural area. Downstairs consisted of four rooms, two on the west and two on the east, separated by a large hallway. Each had a fireplace. Upstairs was one undivided room that ran the entire length and width of the house. All but the north rock wall was plastered over with a lime mixture.

A stairway of stones intricately carved and laid in a half circle led to the kitchen door on the east side of the house. Conrad routed water from Tiger Creek to his house and corral, next to which he built a two-story barn with a pully to lift hay bales to the loft. A boiler provided the steam needed to power the cotton gin, sawmill and gristmill, all built by Conrad.

Despite being the center of a growing community, the couple led a sad life, said Horseshoe Bay resident Jim Jorden, who wrote *A History of the Conrad L. Fuchs Family*, which was published in 2020. "Conrad and his wife split up," Jorden said. "That wasn't common then."

The couple had eight children. The two youngest, Roland B., age three, and Conrad Louis, age five, died of diphtheria in 1878 within a week of each other. "Perhaps the sorrow contributed to the eventual dissolution of Anna's and Conrad's marriage," Jorden wrote in the book, although Anna didn't leave for another eleven years.

When the marriage did dissolve in 1889, Anna moved to San Antonio with her daughters, Lena Marie, twenty-one, and Aldolphina Louise, eighteen, and two sons, Werner J., twenty, and Benjamin Ulysses, seventeen. Son Aldophus Carl or A.C., twenty-three, stayed to work with Conrad, who

Left: Portrait of Anna Fuchs, wife of Conrad Fuchs. *Falls on the Colorado Museum.*

Right: Portrait of Conrad Fuchs. *Falls on the Colorado Museum.*

died nine years later after falling from a pecan tree. Another son, Frederick R., twenty-five, had already left home and was living in Uvalde.

Anna and the children inherited the property, which they sold in 1899, ending the first of what Jorden described in his book as the three eras in the house's saga: the Fuchs Years from 1880 to 1899, the Forgotten Years from 1900 to 1969 and the Horseshoe Bay Years from 1970 to the present.

During the Forgotten Years, the property changed hands ten times, with most owners lasting only a few years before selling again. All the metal and lumber from the mills and other outbuildings were sold off to support the war effort during World War I.

T.M. and J.R. Yett, who bought what was then a 200-acre homestead from Anna and the children, held on for fifteen years, adding around 3,000 acres to the property. The last private owners, Mr. and Mrs. C.T. Hedges, owned the property for twenty-three years, from 1947 to 1970. It was around 850 acres by then.

In 1970, the house entered the Horseshoe Bay Years. Kings Land, Inc., which was owned by Frank King, a nephew of Horseshoe Bay founder and developer Norman Hurd, purchased the house and about 670 acres from the Hedges family.

"The property was assimilated into the Horseshoe Bay Declaration of Reservations in December 1971 and became known as Horseshoe Bay South," Jorden writes. "Thus, the Hurd cousins became aware of the Fuchs House."

Cousins Norman and Wayne Hurd spent $500,000 in 1972 on upgrades to the house, opening it to community events. The Heritage Guild of Horseshoe Bay was founded in 1983 "to bring together those people interested in the history and preservation of historical sites in the Horseshoe Bay area," Jorden wrote. The guild held art shows and holiday open houses regularly throughout the 1980s. However, interest in the guild waned in the 1990s, and it was disbanded.

According to Gary Dilworth, who spent over thirty years working for Horseshoe Bay Resort taking care of landscaping and golf courses, including the land around the Fuchs house, the building was left unlocked for years, drawing late-night revelers. "It got to where it was trashed," he said. "There were beer cans and candle wax everywhere."

Dilworth has fond memories of the place, which he visited often to maintain the grounds and for its peace and tranquility. "I fell in love with it," he said. "There were no houses or anything up there then. It would be just me up there. It was so pretty and untouched."

The house continued to be passed back and forth from the POA to Horseshoe Bay Resort, to SCB Real Estate Investment, to Jaffee Interests, ending up with the City of Horseshoe Bay in 2017.

A dedicated group of volunteers formed the Fuchs House Advisory Committee in 2013 and cleaned up the house and the property. In 2017, they invited the Burnet County Historical Commission for a tour. Pictures taken by Sarah Marie Dilworth (Gary's daughter-in-law) on the day of the tour show the house and its furnishings in good condition.

The property opened for public tours in the first half of 2019, and the advisory committee started raising money to stabilize the aging structure. Their efforts fell short of the $200,000 needed to make the structure safe for public visits. Horseshoe Bay City Manager Jeff Koska said the friends were unable to meet the council's deadline for matching funds to renovate the property.

The city had hired Paul Raley to fix the leaking roof while the fundraising was underway. Paul and his wife, Jennifer, who were living in Pfluggervile, own Raley Design Build, a company that specializes in high-end remodeling projects and historic renovations. When the period for raising the money passed, Horseshoe Bay began looking for a buyer. The Fuchs House was a dream come true for the Raleys.

"The city was looking to get out from underneath it because they were not going to take on the burden of remodeling it," Paul said. "When I found that out, I reached out and started the conversation [about private ownership]."

The Raleys purchased the house and 2.67 acres in 2020 for a symbolic ten dollars and an agreement to follow deed restrictions that include maintenance of the property and public access. The deed also prohibits subdividing the property or selling it. They were in the process of renovating it when embers from a controlled burn caught the roof on fire.

"We loved the house," Jennifer Raley said. "We loved everything about the house. We loved the history of the house. We absolutely were dedicated and committed to preserving and protecting the home. We were proud to be the caretakers of the home. We were really, really looking forward to living in her."

The Raleys had purchased new roofing materials and were waiting for a permit from the City of Horseshoe Bay to begin the work when the house was destroyed. The boxes of fire-resistant roof tiles were stacked in the front yard, unscathed.

The dream of preserving the history of first settlers in the Horseshoe Bay area was not doused with the flames. Plans began immediately to rekindle history from the smoldering embers of oak beams and crumbling rock walls. Pieces of the storied Conrad Fuchs Home are due to become steps to a gazebo on a city hiking trail. Recovered burnt oak beams will be on display in a new city hall, which may also contain a cornerstone rock from the structure. The Raleys' new home will most likely incorporate the locally quarried stone used by a Texas pioneer to shelter his family as they brought industry, education and music to the Hill Country.

The old Fuchs homestead will eventually sport a new historical marker, and placards with historical facts will dot the landscape. The original Texas Historical Commission marker melted in the fire. Even more than 150 years after the first members of the family settled along the Colorado River, the story of their influence is still being written.

"I would like to see the site preserved so that people understand what the Fuchs family did and why it's important for us to know that today," Jorden said. "The house burned, but the message can still be conveyed even if you are looking at ruins."

Esther Ricther Weaver was the sister of the late State Senator Walter Richter and the aunt of Senator Richter's daughter Robyn Richter, who still lives on the family's Double Horn Ranch in Marble Falls.

Chapter 2

THE LEGEND OF NOAH SMITHWICK COMES TO LIFE

Noah Smithwick lived a life as big as Texas history. A Texas Ranger, gunsmith, blacksmith, miller and memoirist, Smithwick helped shape the history of the Lone Star State, including Burnet County. His memoir, *The Evolution of a State: Recollections of Old Texas Days*, was written in the pioneer's final years, six decades after he left Burnet County for the safety of California during the Civil War. It was first published in 1900 by Gammel Book Company but is now in the public domain and can be found in many different editions, including one by the University of Texas Press.

History buff Charles Watkins of Marble Falls used his well-worn copy to research his script when he portrayed Smithwick in Legends of the Falls, a theatrical hayride through history event held in Cottonwood Shores in 2021, 2022 and 2023. He portrayed Smithwick in 2023, the last year the event was held.

"I have always just adored Noah Smithwick," Watkins said. "He's always been one of my heroes."

Smithwick was born in 1808 in Martin County, North Carolina. The family, which included stonemasons of Scottish descent, moved to Tennessee. In 1827, young Noah migrated to Texas.

"What the discovery of gold was to California, the colonization act of 1825 was to Texas," reads the very first line in Smithwick's twenty-six-chapter book.

Left: A photograph of Noah Smithwick taken in Santa Ana, California. *DeGolyer Library, Southern Methodist University.*

Right: Charles Watkins of Marble Falls as Noah Smithwick holding a Bowie knife in the 2023 Legends of the Falls theatrical hayride in Cottonwood Shores. *The Picayune Magazine.*

He continues to describe a promised land with woods that "abounded in bee trees, wild grapes, plums, cherries, persimmons, hews, and dewberries, while walnuts, hickory nuts, and pecans were abundant along the water courses."

"The climate was so mild that houses were not essential," he continued. "Neither was a superabundance of clothing or bedding; buffalo robes and bear skins supply all that was needed for the latter and buckskin the former."

Smithwick's life covered many of Texas's most historic moments. Davy Crockett recruited him to fight at the Alamo, but after a winter in the woods, Smithwick was ill and in a hospital near death. Crockett rode on to San Antonio without him.

He counted many of the state's founding fathers as good friends, including Sam Houston, the first and third president of the Republic of Texas, and David G. Burnet, the interim president of Texas, vice president of the Republic of Texas and secretary of state when it was accepted into the Union.

Smithwick lived with Stephen F. Austin for a time and made Jim Bowie's replacement knife after the famous fighter had his renowned and deadly weapon filigreed for posterity after the Sandbar Fight near Natchez in 1827. Smithwick claims he created a duplicate of the knife at Bowie's request when he worked as a blacksmith in San Felipe de Austin. He was not the only person to make that claim, as the knife was popular. Smithwick began mass-producing Bowie knives and made quite a bit of money, according to his memoir. "Smithwick made the one Bowie fought with at the Alamo," Watkins said.

As he polished his script for the fall 2023 event, Watkins marveled at how Smithwick's experiences changed the man. He fought with the Texans and the Texas Rangers against Native Americans, mainly to reclaim property stolen from white settlers. His views of these first Americans changed after he spent eight months with a Comanche tribe outside the Bastrop area.

"He got to be the adopted son of the chief and became a part of their daily lives," Watkins said when asked what inspired him most about Smithwick. "Up until then, he had been anti–Native American, but in Bastrop, he was sent to negotiate a peace treaty. But of course, he came back, and they [white settlers] pulled out of the treaty."

Smithwick moved to Fort Croghan in Burnet, where he became armorer to the U.S. Army Second Dragoons. He quickly made friends with Logan Vandeveer, who sold meat to the soldiers. In fact, his nephew married one of Vandeveer's daughters (more on that coming up).

He also became friendly with Lyman Wight and a band of Mormon families who built a mill on Hamilton Creek. Smithwick helped pave the way for the group with other residents in the area who were skeptical of the religion and lifestyle. "Smithwick got to know them," Watkins said. "He introduced them into the city [Marble Falls] and helped people get comfortable with the idea they were Mormons."

The Mormons were negotiating with state leaders to set up a community for their people, bands of whom were steadily moving west looking for a permanent home. As the Civil War approached, the Mormons, who were abolitionists, decided it would be best to move along and sold their mill to Smithwick. "If they had stayed, Marble Falls might have been a second Salt Lake City," Watkins said with a mischievous grin. "How could they resist Granite Mountain as their temple?"

Smithwick, too, was forced out of the area because of his abolitionist views. "As the son of a revolutionary soldier, I could not raise my hand against the Union he had fought to establish," Smithwick said he told Houston. "I had fought to make Texas a member of the Union, and I would not turn round and fight to undo my work."

When the Ordinance of Secession passed in Texas, Smithwick sold his farm and turned his mill over to his nephew John Hubbard, who had decided to stay. Hubbard was married to Eliza Vandeveer and living in what is now known as the Bluebonnet House, which can still be seen on U.S. 281 north in Marble Falls. Death threats prompted Hubbard to decide to leave, but bushwhackers intercepted and murdered him. His body was thrown into a watering hole at Cow Creek, which was subsequently named Hubbard Falls in remembrance.

Smithwick lived out the rest of his life in the Golden State. He died in Santa Ana, Orange County, in Southern California in 1899 at the age of ninety-one.

Watkins, with his long gray beard and imposing height, worked to make his hero proud in the four minutes he had to deliver the story of a state.

Chapter 3

FAMILIES OF THE BLUEBONNET HOUSE

Bluebonnet season never fails to highlight one of Burnet County's historic gems: a 170-year-old building on U.S. 281 in north Marble Falls known as the Bluebonnet House.

"It's such an icon," said Burnet resident Tommye Potts, whose grandfather Christian Dorbandt Jr. was born in the house in 1857. "This house is known worldwide. I've seen pictures of it on everything. I've even seen a shower curtain with this house on it."

In late March and early April of most years, a vibrant field of bluebonnets separates the stone house and barn from the highway. The acreage is surrounded by a barbed-wire fence, where spectators line up to take photos during the height of bluebonnet season.

The Dorbandts were the second family to own the property by deed, which included 212 acres, but no one is quite sure who built the house or, at least, the original part in the center. Two additions were added over the years.

One school of thought is that Logan Vandeveer built the center section on land granted to him by the newly formed Republic of Texas to use as his ranch headquarters. His family of four daughters lived in Burnet to be near school. His wife died sometime around 1850, but no grave or record has been found of her death, according to the Texas State Historical Association. More than two thousand acres of land, including the property where the Bluebonnet House now stands, was given to Vandeveer for his participation

The Bluebonnet House on U.S. 281 in Marble Falls in the spring of 2022. *Dakota Morrissiey.*

as a soldier in the Texas Revolution. He was wounded at the Battle of San Jacinto, where Texas won its independence from Mexico.

Many, including Potts, believe the house was built by Christian Dorbandt Sr., her great-grandfather, who was stationed with the U.S. Army Second Dragoon Regiment at Fort Croghan in Burnet. Dorbandt Sr. emigrated from Denmark at the age of sixteen. He joined the U.S. Army and fought in the Mexican War, receiving a Certificate of Merit from President James K. Polk for his role in the Battle of Cerro Gordo. He served as quartermaster sergeant at Fort Croghan in what was then known as Hamilton Valley (now Burnet).

During the Civil War, Dorbandt Sr. was a captain in the Confederate army. He moved his family from the Bluebonnet House to Smithwick and then to San Gabriel near Bertram, where he built a gin and saloon. The enterprises went out of business when residents voted the precinct dry in 1878. He was a captain in the Texas Rangers and was recognized posthumously in a Texas Memorial Cross Service at South San Gabriel Cemetery. He died in 1910.

Dorbandt and his Irish wife, Annie Dunlavy, are believed to be the first family to call the house home.

"As I grew up, all my family has always said that Captain Dorbandt built that house," Potts said.

Burnet County Sheriff Christian Dorbandt Jr. and his wife, Anna Perkins, stand in the doorway of the Burnet County Jail. (Others not identified.) *Tommye Dorbandt Potts.*

Three of Christian and Annie's fourteen children were born in the Bluebonnet House, including Potts's grandfather Christian Jr. Their first child, Henrietta, was the first white female born in the county, just two months after the first white male, George Holland. Holland was born in October 1853, and Henrietta in December of that year.

Dorbandt Jr. was a cattle driver and rancher before going into law enforcement. He was the Burnet city marshal for two years and served as a deputy sheriff for eighteen months before he was elected Burnet County sheriff, a job he held for eight years. He and his wife, Anna R. Perkins, had ten children.

According to Potts's aunt Rethie Dorbandt, the house was built with slave labor. "At the time, there was a Black stonemason named Primus Lewis," Potts said. "He built the chimneys, and she thinks it's likely he built the house, too."

The Dorbandts moved into the house in 1853, the year it was built. Records show that Vandeveer sold 212 acres, including the house, to Dorbandt and Theodore Winkle, another soldier at Fort Croghan, in February 1855. Potts has a copy of the recorded, handwritten deed with Vandeveer's signature. A second recorded copy has "Satisfied deed" written across it.

Soon after selling the property, Vandeveer and his brother Zachary set off on a cattle drive to Louisiana, where he counted on selling enough beef cows to pay off a $6,000 debt he owed Fort Croghan's last commander, Lieutenant Newton C. Givens. Vandeveer made his living selling beef to the fort, but when it closed, he had to find a new source of income, which is why he and Zachary hit the cattle trail to New Orleans.

By September 1855, the brothers were dead, victims of yellow fever. Logan was forty years old and Zachary was thirty-six.

Vandeveer had no will and left behind four orphaned daughters, ages sixteen, fourteen, nine and six, who were now in debt and homeless. "They [the daughters] wanted the land and the house," Potts said. "What I think is that my great-grandfather walked away from it. He was an honorable man and always said he was proud that he and his children had never done anything to end up in court. The [Vandeveer] daughters were orphans. Everything was tied up in court. Rather than go to court, he just walked away."

Eliza and her sisters moved into what was then known as the Dorbandt House. Eliza married John Randolph Hubbard in 1856, when she was seventeen. Hubbard was the nephew of another local historic figure of note, Noah Smithwick.

Like Smithwick, Hubbard was a known supporter of the Union during the Civil War (1861–65). Smithwick had already left for the safety of California when Hubbard decided to follow. He didn't get far. In 1863, at the height of the war, bushwhackers captured and killed him, throwing his body into what is still known as Hubbard Falls on Cow Creek northeast of Smithwick.

In 1869, Eliza exchanged houses with her sister Emily Christian. Only three years later, Emily sold the house to N.A. Cavin, passing it out of the Vandeveer family's hands for good. Cavin is believed to have built the eastern addition.

Cavin sold the home in 1889 to Fielding Harper Holloway, an entrepreneur who put up the first telephone and telegraph lines between Lampasas, Burnet, Austin and Marble Falls. He was instrumental in bringing the railroad to the area and also built the state's first tannery and boot factory in Marble Falls.

The next owner was rancher Ernest Herman Odiorne, who bought the property in 1905. He died eleven years later from an accidental self-inflicted gunshot wound while crawling through a barbed-wire fence.

Before his death, he sold the property to his brother James Eben Odiorne. That was in 1908.

In 1911, Odiorne sold to Charles F. Konvicka, an Austrian native. He and his wife, Anna Mican Konvicka, also from Austria, had ten children. Two of those children, Anton and Angeline, were living in the house when Potts first visited it with her mother at the age of eleven. The Konvicka siblings were the last family to ever live there.

"I was just amazed at it," Potts said of her visit in 1960. "Those people lived very simply. They had a table and chair and two beds in the main room by the fireplace. I remember there was a package of cereal, just dried cereal and canned milk, on that table. They were very nice to me and welcomed us in."

Legend has it that Charles Konvicka built a car inside the house and then couldn't get it out. Potts said she saw no car on the property, but according to a 2020 magazine article, a relative said Charles bought a car but couldn't drive. He never registered the vehicle, so his sons removed the tires and put the car on blocks in the barn.

Angeline died in 1973 and Anton in 1975. A year later, the house was sold in an estate sale to the Atkinson family.

Potts returned to the house in 2013 with the Burnet County Historical Commission for a tour.

"We saw then it was deteriorating," she said. "It was full of old appliances and garbage."

Several members of the commission hope to someday have a subject marker placed on Texas Department of Transportation property along the highway near the house.

"We deal with history and historical buildings, and we'd like to honor it," commission Chair Rachel Bryson said. "The Bluebonnet House has been in *Texas Monthly*; it's been all over the place. The commission hopes to someday have a marker near there to explain the history of the house and give it the recognition it deserves."

Chapter 4

DESCENDANT DAUGHTERS OF FIRST SETTLER STILL RANCHING

Ranching is "a heritage thing" to sisters Donna Holland Wilcox and Meredith Holland Clowdus of Marble Falls. Their mixed Charolais, Black Angus and Brahman cows are descendants of a herd that began in 1947, when their grandparents Malcolm and Louise Holland began ranching.

That particular piece of property on CR 341 off Mormon Mill Road is surrounded by other working Holland ranches, all of which go back six generations to Samuel Eli Holland, a man with deep roots in Burnet County history.

"Samuel Holland was the first settler in Burnet County," Wilcox said. "He bought 1,240 acres for forty-seven cents an acre. He bred the first white-faced cattle that became a legacy cattle in this area."

Those cattle were some of the first Herefords in Texas.

Samuel E. Holland, Donna and Meredith's great-great-great-grandfather, purchased his considerable acreage along Hamilton Creek on July 3, 1848. Within a week, he had moved his wagon of worldly goods from where he was camping on what is now the state capitol grounds to his new homestead. He went from chopping cedar for houses in Austin to clearing land and building a log cabin to live in, the first permanent home in the area.

The Burnet County pioneer strung the first wire fence and built the first all-stone home in the area, according to *Types of Successful Men of Texas* by Lewis E. Daniel, a book published by printer E. Von Boeckmann in 1890. Holland fought in the Mexican-American War and was a colonel in the Civil War.

Sisters Meredith Clowdus (*left*) and Donna Wilcox ranch the land settled by their great-great-great-grandfather Samuel E. Holland, a first settler in Burnet County. *Suzanne Freeman.*

Although he fought for the Confederacy, he lent his considerable military skills to stopping the persecution of Union supporters locally. Burnet County voted 96 percent against secession from the United States, but some Confederate voices were loud and their actions brazen and even murderous. Vigilantes were known to throw Unionists into Dead Man's Hole near Marble Falls. Holland was part of a team of citizens who brought law and order back to the area.

During his ninety-one years, he served as a state representative, county commissioner and county treasurer.

While the Holland family has sold some of their ancestor's original acreage, most of it has stayed in family hands. Wilcox, Clowdus and their father, Don Holland, all have homes on contiguous ranch land where they raise livestock together for the Holland Cattle and Sheep Company. The sheep stay on one side of the ranch, where the land is rockier, while the cattle graze on the other side, where coastal grasses grow on flat, fertile soil. Holland beef is grass-fed only. They sell it at auctions and to local families. The sheep are also raised for meat and sold year-round.

"It's important to remain grass-fed—our ranch is based on grass-fed meat," Clowdus said. "It's healthier for us and for our customers." Grass is key to ranching, both said.

"If you don't manage your grass and you have to feed, you don't make any money," Wilcox said. "You don't make a lot of money off ranching anyway. You don't want to waste the money you do make on buying feed."

They are passing those skills and the family passion for ranching on to their own daughters, who each plan to take over ranching duties from their mothers once they are out of school. The one male in the mix of siblings and cousins is a rodeo bull rider and horse trainer.

Meredith and Donna also have a brother, Todd Holland, who owns Holland Surveying in Marble Falls. He leaves the ranching to his sisters, Wilcox said.

Their husbands, Canyon Clowdus and Brad Wilcox, have full-time jobs elsewhere as well. Meredith and Donna call them, along with their dad, "the muscles of the operation." The men help with land maintenance chores and predator control.

Family history turns up at almost every curve along the ATV trails that wind through the rocks, cactus, grass and wildflowers that cover the ranch land. The four-wheel-drive bumps over gray, rocky terrain where stagecoaches and wagons once traveled, guided along by ancient wooden beams held in place with rusty railroad spikes.

Trails lead on past a pecan bottom, the proceeds of which were used by their grandparents to buy the land.

"They also sold goats and worked at Texas Granite [quarry]," Wilcox said of grandparents Malcolm and Louise. "My grandmother worked at the schools. They were never not working."

Hamilton Creek hooks through the property and back, giving them four shorelines on a valuable resource. The land, the lessons, the memories and history are all part of the Holland heritage that the females in the family plan on maintaining and growing into the future.

"It's an ecosystem and a balance," Wilcox said of raising families and livestock on family land. "The product is healthy meat and legacy."

Chapter 5

FACT VERSUS FICTION IN A TALL TALE OF LOGAN VANDEVEER

H e is described as a "noble figure" of "splendid physique" dressed in a deerskin suit riding a black war horse through Burnet County to rescue a fair maiden from violent kidnappers. Logan Vandeveer was a true Texican hero, but the story you are about to read is more dime-store Western than carefully researched biography. The following is a mixture of fact and fiction, so read with discernment.

FACT

Vandeveer (1815–1855) was a Texas revolutionary soldier, a Texas Ranger and a founding father of Burnet County, where he served as the community's first postmaster, built its first school and its first stone building (still in use as the Masonic Lodge in Burnet) and became its first merchant.

He was granted two partial leagues of land in Central Texas as a reward for his participation in the Battle of San Jacinto. The Congress of the Republic of Texas reclaimed one parcel of that land for a capitol building. The eminent domain seizure included much of what is now downtown Austin.

The second grant was in Burnet County, where Vandeveer raised cattle to provide meat to the soldiers at Fort Croghan, built to provide protection to white settlers. When the fort closed in 1853, he and his brother Zachary

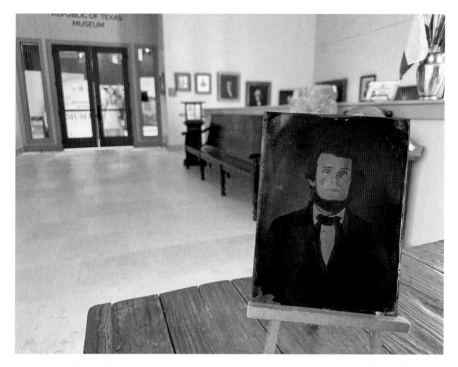

A tintype of Logan Vandeveer in the archives of the Daughters of the Republic of Texas Museum in Austin. It is not usually on display. *Suzanne Freeman.*

had to find customers elsewhere. In 1855, they herded their stock to sell at auction in Plaquemines Parish, Louisiana, where they both died of yellow fever.

Vandeveer died at forty, only six years after moving to Burnet County, where his was one of eighty signatures officially establishing the county and becoming one of its first county commissioners. He left a lasting legacy in his new home and in the state of Texas, as well as in the works of Wild West melodrama.

MOSTLY FICTION

A Burnet County "news feature writer" named Mary Johnson Posey wrote three versions of the following tall tale that was originally printed in an Austin newspaper. It can be heard to this day on a guided tour of Longhorn Cavern.

Mary Johnson Posey* wrote the story, which was first published in the February 24, 1918, edition of the *Austin American* (not yet the *Austin American-Statesman*). She cast Vandeveer and two companions, W.H. Magill and Noah Smithwick, also of Burnet County, as frontier heroes who saved a fragile heroine from a band of Native Americans she labeled "savages."

"This is the vivid story of Logan Van Deveer** [sic], at one time owner of the townsite of the city of Austin, and who rescued from the Indians the fairest belle of San Antonio, whom he afterward married," reads the first sentence in Posey's missive. "Van Deveer was a hero of San Jacinto's bloody battlefield. The story also tells of a terrific fight with Indians in Burnet County. It is a story for all Texans to know, a story historically authentic and taken from historical records."

The fight and rescue of "fairest belle of San Antonio" Mariel King is said to have begun at the historic Council House Fight in San Antonio. Before getting to that, however, it is important to point out that Mariel King did not marry Vandeveer, who was already married to Lucinda Mayes at the time.

Logan and Lucinda had seven children together in Bastrop before moving with their four daughters to Burnet. Lucinda died shortly after the 1850 census, though no official record or burial site has ever been found. That was ten years after the Council House Fight, so the couple was still building a family when King was rescued.

The claim of "historically authentic facts" taken from "historical records" did not make it into the two versions printed years later in the *Frontier Times*, first in April 1926 and again in June 1938.

In the earlier version in the *Times*, the story had a new focus: Sherrard's Cave, now known as Longhorn Cavern. Posey wrote that she had no documented proof of the account's authenticity but that she heard it from an original Burnet settler of "highest honor and integrity." "And while it is not recorded in history, I am sure that it is true, as these men were his [Vandeveer's] personal friends in the early days," she wrote.

She does not reveal her own connection to the early settlers, which might have lent more credibility to her story, as it is a close one. Posey was the daughter of Marble Falls founder Confederate General Adam R. Johnson, who was integral in trading the stone from Granite Mountain used to build the capitol for a rail line.

The Council House Fight occurred in 1840 in San Antonio between Texas troops and Penateka Comanche leaders. According to Posey, Vandeveer was there as part of the military.

According to the Texas Historical Association, peaceful negotiations over the return of settlers held hostage by Comanches turned into a bloody battle, resulting in the deaths of thirty Native American leaders and warriors and five women and children. Twenty-seven Comanches were captured but escaped as soldiers attempted to exchange them for the still missing white captives.

According to Posey's first version, which was reprinted almost word for word in the *Frontier Times* in 1938, the escaping Comanches grabbed King and headed north into Burnet County.

In the second telling of the story, printed in 1926, she introduces a specific villain, Chief Yellow Wolf, who, she writes, had seen Mariel King "and then and there marked her for his own." Yellow Wolf began repeated attacks on San Antonio, eventually capturing thirteen settlers. When he realized King was not among them, "he swore a terrible oath that he would get her in spite of everything," the story reads. According to Posey, this led to the ill-fated negotiations and the Council House Fight.

Posey follows this with a brutal, although somewhat comic, scene of hand-to-hand combat by two men on horseback—on the same horse. As Vandeveer sat atop his black charger watching the negotiations, a Comanche named Red Fox jumped up behind him and "pinioned his [Vandeveer's] arms to his sides while he [Red Fox] kicked the black horse's sides viciously, sending him into a wild run." Vandeveer managed to maintain control of the horse, steering it in circles. The scene drew a crowd, and eventually, someone shot and killed Red Fox.

On his way home after the battle, Vandeveer found a looted wagon train and evidence that a woman had been kidnapped. He followed a trail marked by a dropped lacy handkerchief and later a bit of ribbon into Marble Falls, where he enlisted his friends Smithwick and Magill to help rescue the woman. The three found Mariel King tied and leaning against stone in Sherrard's Cave (Longhorn Cavern).

"Even in the dishevelment of her capture and subsequent journey with her captors, the girl was beautiful, and though her dark wavy hair hung in a tangled mass, her lustrous brown eyes held weariness with despair, she was still lovely enough to be the belle of the Alamo City," Posey wrote.

Vandeveer and company fired on the unsuspecting kidnappers who fled, thinking they were outnumbered. One stayed behind and was about to kill King when Vandeveer stopped him in what was described as a bloody hand-to-hand battle.

The kidnappers soon realized only three men had attacked them, and they returned to the scene, where they attempted to scalp the young woman as they battled the three pioneers. Vandeveer and his companions prevailed and saved the damsel in distress, a scene described at some length in terms both bloody and bigoted. The end is a Wild West version of meet-cute.

"Van Deveer now caught up the fainting girl in his powerful arms, and with Magill and Smithwick protecting his retreat, he climbed up the rocky passageway leading out of the cave and soon reached their horses safely," the story continues. "Of course, the natural sequel to this rescue was marriage," she writes inaccurately in conclusion.

In the original 1918 version, Posey ends the story with a final paragraph of purple prose.

"Though Texas' heraldic roll glows with the names of Houston, McCulloch, Hays, Lamar, and Chevalier, which illumines the pages of her history with an effulgence of glory, she never nurtured on her bosom a son of more filial devotion or indomitable will to do and dare, or of more loyal patriotism than Logan Van Deveer, original owner of Austin, who now rests 'on Fame's Eternal Camping Ground,'" she concludes.

The tale is still told today during tours of the underground at Longhorn Cavern State Park, although it is a much shorter version. "We don't mention anyone by name," Longhorn Cavern general manager Jimmy Cruz said. "We just talk about the incident itself. We say that some Texas Rangers rescued a girl being held captive by some Native Americans inhabiting the cave."

*The author Mary Johnson Posey (1884–1960) is buried in the Old Burnet Cemetery (former Old Fellows Cemetery). She was known as a newspaper feature writer.

**Vandeveer's name is spelled various ways in stories and even on street signs, but the commonly accepted version is Vandeveer, which shows up on most historical documents. That's Vandeveer NOT VandERveer, which is how it is spelled on a prominent street in Burnet, a seemingly accepted misspelling that no one seems eager to change.

Chapter 6

MADAME MAYOR

Promising to "make two nickels grow where only one grew before," Ophelia "Birdie" Harwood became mayor of Marble Falls three years before the Nineteenth Amendment granted women the right to vote. Elected in 1917, she was the first female mayor in the state and the first in the United States to be seated by an all-male electorate. Later, in 1936, she became the first woman to serve as a municipal court judge.

Although mayor for only two years, Harwood left a lasting legacy in the river city. She ran a campaign ad in the *Marble Falls Messenger* titled "Why I Am Running for Mayor of Marble Falls," published on March 15, 1917. In April of that year, she won the election by a vote of seventy-nine to thirty-three.

Here are a few excerpts from her lengthy statement in the paper:

> *A woman's first duty is to her home and children: when she has raised them up to take their place in the world, it is then her duty to turn to her State and there help make and enforce the laws that will make it a fit abiding place for them.*
>
> *If elected Mayor, I shall expect every man connected with this office to do his whole duty with this for our goal—"A bigger and more progressive Marble Falls."*
>
> *…We stand for morality, sobriety and, above all, for justice, and if elected our humblest citizens will be treated with the same regard as others.*

Mayor Ophelia "Birdie" Harwood travels by horse on Main Street in downtown Marble Falls. *Falls on the Colorado Museum.*

We are not going to increase the tax rate, only by vote of the people.
We are going to be very careful how we spend the peoples' money. We are going to try to make two nickels grow where only one grew before.
If I am elected Mayor of Marble Falls, our books will always be open for inspection. Semi-annually our receipts and expenditures will be published in the Messenger.

Her platform included promises to clean up the town by keeping cattle penned in and off the streets and drunks at home or in jail and out of the gutters.

During her tenure, Mayor Harwood convinced city commissioners to approve a rule that drivers should honk when turning corners and keep to the right of turning posts in the streets. This was to cut down on drunken driver incidents. She also supported keeping the oak trees that shaded Main Street. Eventually, voters won out, and the trees that ran down the middle of Main were cut down, but not during Harwood's tenure. Also, Marble Falls was upgraded from "town" to "city," indicating the continual growth of the community.

Four days after her election on April 2, 1917, the United States officially joined Britain, France and Russia in World War I. All three of her sons fought in the war. For her part, she sponsored a fundraising drive for clothing for European Jewish war refugees. Along with Edith Darragh, she also organized a local chapter of the American Red Cross to collect donations for the war effort.

According to one of her granddaughters, Nell Harwood Holmes of Yuba City, California, she similarly influenced her large family. Holmes, who died in 2017 at the age of ninety-five, wrote a six-page homage to her grandparents Dr. and Mrs. George Hill Harwood. Written in 1993, her anecdotes run from nostalgic to celebratory to tragic. A copy of the letter can be found at the Falls on the Colorado Museum in the Old Granite School House, 2001 Broadway in Marble Falls.

An accomplished equestrian, Harwood claimed to have been riding horses since before she could walk. Named "Birdie" because of her small size when she was born, Harwood was given provisions and tied to a horse as a child to roam loose in the outdoors "for her health," according to her granddaughter.

During the few years Holmes lived in Marble Falls, she recalls Harwood piling five of her grandchildren into the one-passenger seat in her Wileys-Overland Whippet automobile to drive them to school. "Every day, I mean every day, we were five minutes late," Holmes wrote. "We would spill out when we reached the school, dash over the stile and sprint for the front door."

In all other matters of social life, Grannyma and Granddad were sticklers for propriety. Dr. Harwood "was a very proper Englishman," according to Holmes. "He had always come to the table to eat in a full suit, including vest," she recalled. His table manners "bordered on perfection."

Grannyma often called her four granddaughters to her bedroom in the mornings for lectures on modesty. "She had a shocking remonstrance for the girls," Holmes wrote. "'Don't you ever let some man take advantage of you—or your Dad'll have to kill him!'"

Dr. and Mrs. Harwood's home was known as Liberty Hall, which still stands at 119 Avenue G and is now a business office.

Perhaps one of the most famous stories attached to Birdie Harwood and Liberty Hall involves a young teacher who delivered milk to the house as a second job. One day, Harwood presented him with a microscope for his class. "The young man became the future President of the United States of America—Lyndon Baines Johnson," Holmes recalls. She was standing in the living room when the transaction took place. "Embarrassingly, I was dressed in shorts," she wrote.

Holmes also recalled the day her brother Charles and friend J.B. Cox walked down a steep path to the river. Fascinated by the huge catfish they could see swimming near the surface, Charles leaned over and fell in. Cox saved him by extending a "stout stick" out into the current, which Charles grabbed to be pulled back to shore.

"Grannyma was so shaken when we told her that she told us to find a long switch," Holmes wrote. "Previously, she had warned us not to go to the river. She had explained how she had combed sand out of the hair of young girls who Dr. Harwood had tried to resuscitate and how Uncle George had dived in the river to bring out drowned persons."

Those drownings had such an effect on Harwood that when she became mayor, she had warning signs erected near the most dangerous areas of the river. This was before the dams were built, forming the Highland Lakes.

Tragedy struck the family a number of times. Dr. and Birdie Harwood had four sons: Gerald, George, Francis and Clarence. Francis died at the age of six months.

In his later years, Dr. Harwood was injured helping rescue several young people from a car crash on the steep hill south of the river (now U.S. 281). He never recovered despite the devoted attention of his family, including his son George, who spent most of his life at his father's side.

"He and Uncle George were great friends as well as father and son," Holmes wrote. "How fortunate to have such a great relationship. Uncle George had devoted much of his adult life to driving for Granddad."

George was devastated by his father's injury. He was especially disturbed that the family could not afford an expensive treatment he believed would keep his father alive. "Uncle George took his own life in hopes that proceeds from his WWI G.I. insurance would provide the funds [for treatment]," according to Holmes. "Sadly, Dr. Harwood died a few weeks later. Life would never be the same for the doctor's wife."

Birdie Harwood lived many more years after her husband, eventually remarrying a childhood sweetheart, Bob Beverly. The couple lived in Johnson City, where she died in 1954.

"There are many things more to be said and some to be unsaid," Holmes wrote in conclusion. "But the lives of these exceptional grandparents of mine complemented each other in ways to benefit those whose lives they touched. Dedication is the word their lives personified."

FAMILY CONNECTIONS (1872–1954)

- Ophelia "Birdie" Harwood was the granddaughter of Stephen Crosby, the first elected land commissioner of Texas. He served from 1851 to 1858.
- Her father, Charles Adolphus Crosby, traveled with General Albert Sydney Johnson, exploring remote frontier forts in Texas.
- Her mother, Eliza Greene, was related to President Grover Cleveland and to General Israel Putnam, who was so close to General George Washington that the nation's first president used to say if anything happened to him, he wanted "Old Put" to take over.
- Dr. Harwood was born in England. He graduated from the University of Edinburgh in Scotland before coming to the United States. He met his future wife in Johnson City, where she lived at the time.

A formal portrait of Marble Falls Mayor Ophelia "Birdie" Harwood. Several of her dresses are on display in the Falls on the Colorado Museum. *Falls on the Colorado Museum.*

- The boat that Dr. Harwood traveled on from England to Texas split in half during a fierce storm. He washed up on the shores of Galveston with several other survivors. They were rescued by the American Red Cross.
- Ophelia "Birdie" Crosby married Dr. George Harwood in 1892 in Blanco County. They settled in Marble Falls immediately after.
- Birdie is buried in the Marble Falls Cemetery along with her husband, Dr. George Harwood, who died in 1934; one of her sons, George Harwood, who died in 1933; and her mother, Ophelia Cleveland Crosby (Mrs. Charles Adolphus Crosby).

PART III

LAW AND DISORDER

Chapter 1

CRIMINAL MYSTERY

The outlaw Jesse James might have lived a short time at the Roper Hotel in Marble Falls. Or maybe it was Frank Dalton, a U.S. marshal whose brothers rode with the Cole Younger and Jesse James gangs robbing trains and banks in the late 1800s. Or maybe he was someone else altogether.

Described as a big man with a gray beard, the stranger registered under the name J. Frank Dalton sometime in the early 1940s. He stayed through a fall and a winter, leaving room 7 each day to walk downtown and sell war bonds. When he came home in the evenings, other guests gathered around to hear him read his stories, all of which he claimed were true.

The man everyone called Frank kept his handwritten and typed tales in a trunk in his second-floor room at the top of the stairs. Those stories, including "The Civil War and Its Aftermath," "We Meet the Pinkertons" and "Belle Starr," all now reside in the Dolph Briscoe Center for American History at the University of Texas at Austin.

When Dalton eventually left Marble Falls, he left behind his trunk of stories. Hazel Smith Ingram, whose family owned the Roper when Dalton was staying there, eventually donated the trunk's contents to the Marble Falls library, which, at the time, was run by Marie Ebeling Houy out of a room in the old Masonic lodge. When Houy retired, library staff told her to take the papers with her. In 1979, she gave them to the Briscoe Center.

The trunk also contained tintypes of a woman purported to be Belle Starr, the Bandit Queen, and a man he said was himself, U.S. Marshal Frank

Dalton. In his version of the story, he was part of the marauders before changing his life and becoming a marshal. He also claimed Starr was a childhood friend and long-lost love.

Each of the yellowed, typed pages has the name "Frank Dalton" in the upper-left-hand corner. Edges are worn from handling, and the typing is edited in places with light pencil marks.

Written in the purple prose of a dime-store novel, the stories sometimes read like fact, sometimes fiction. Most are in first person. The language is brutally racist, and all stories are pro-Confederacy. All protagonists are

The outlaw Jesse James. *Public domain.*

victims of the injustices of Union soldiers. His obvious prejudices might be why the local library wanted no part of his papers.

In "The Civil War and Its Aftermath," Dalton begins: "My people were from Georgia, where they had settled during the Revolutionary War." This story tells of how he and members of his family joined up with Quantrill's Raiders, also called Quantrill's Militia or bushwhackers, during the Civil War. (Dalton spelled the name Quantrell.) The bushwhackers practiced guerrilla warfare and were not official Confederate soldiers.

Included in William Quantrill's gang were the James boys, the Youngers and the Daltons. According to a PBS documentary, Quantrill taught the up-and-coming gangsters the tactics they used during robberies, so this much at least appears to be true.

"We Meet the Pinkertons" continues a portrayal of reluctant outlaws with hearts of gold. They cornered four Pinkerton detectives who were following them as they rode "to visit our mother and sisters—to see them for the first time since the war closed." Holding the men at gunpoint, they explained why they would not kill them.

"This is not the way we do things, so I guess we'll have to let you go," the story reads. "You go back to your chief in Chicago and tell him to quit sending men out to hunt us. We are not criminals but were outlawed at the close of the war for trying to protect our homes."

A five-thousand-word piece on Belle Starr depicts a misunderstood mother and rancher who could never do wrong. He describes each of her multiple men—some she married, some she did not—as unjustly criminalized by war.

According to historical records, Belle Starr was born in Missouri but began her life of crime after the war when she moved to Texas and fell in with the James-Younger gang. Trained in piano and schooled in the classics, she wore velvet skirts and plumed hats when riding out to rustle cattle and rob trains. Myra Belle Shirley took her famous name from Sam Starr, a Cherokee she met after being chased to Oklahoma by the Texas Rangers, although she and Sam never officially married. The couple spent nine months in prison for stealing horses, an event that Dalton describes as a misunderstanding between her and a neighboring rancher, whose lost horse looked identical to hers.

Little of what Dalton wrote about Starr resembles anything found in official records. His magnum opus ends mid-sentence as Dalton rides off into the sunset after a short reunion with his one true love. A handwritten addendum reads:

> *On February 3rd 1889 Belle was shot from her horse and killed. One side of her face was literally shot to pieces by a load of buck shot fired from ambush. Her murderer was never apprehended.*
>
> *Thus passed from a sad and turbulent life "Belle Starr" on the evening of her 43rd birthday. Some there are who called her an Outlaw, but to me who knew her well, she will ever be remembered as a true, staunch and faithful friend, and loyal and beloved comrade. Just another victim of the grim horrors and unspeakable terrors and hardships of war.*
>
> *She lies buried in a neglected and weed grown mound near her log cabin home at Briar Town in the wilds of the Old Indian Territory, perhaps a fit resting place for a Pioneer woman of the old—and lawless—frontier.*
>
> *Rest in peace beloved comrade. Days of hate and strife are over. Rest in peace, ere long I'll join you on that bright and happy shore.*

J. Frank Dalton died in 1951 at the age of 103 in Granbury, Texas. He lived his final years as part of a traveling act—his role to show audiences a maimed finger, rope burns on his neck, fire burns on his feet and thirty-two bullet wounds in his chest to prove he was indeed Jesse James.

Dalton's gravestone in Granbury reads, "Jesse Woodson James, Supposedly killed in 1882." According to historical records, Jesse James was killed at the age of thirty-four by fellow gang member Robert Ford. He is buried in Kearney, Missouri.

In an attempt to clear the record, both graves were exhumed: James's in 1995, Dalton's in 2000. DNA tests proved the remains in Missouri were those of Jesse James. Two bodies were found in the Granbury grave, but only one was tested. It belonged to a man who died in 1927, neither Jesse James nor J. Frank Dalton.

One final problem with the story of the mysterious lodger at the Roper Hotel: U.S. Marshal Frank Dalton, who was never a former bank robber, was killed in the line of duty on November 27, 1887. He is buried in Elmwood Cemetery in Coffeyville, Kansas, where two of his four outlaw brothers also rest in peace.

The confusion over identity comes from unsubstantiated claims that James faked his death and moved to Texas to live out his life, perhaps spending part of it selling war bonds and spinning tales to lodgers in the Roper Hotel in Marble Falls.

Chapter 2

AT HOME IN THE BURNET COUNTY JAIL

Vonnie Riddell Fox celebrated her ninety-eighth birthday in August 2024 in jail. The public celebration was held in the Old Burnet County Jail, which was her family home from when she was thirteen to twenty-four years old. She was never a prisoner. She was one of four children of Sheriff Wallace Riddell and his wife (and jail matron), Rachel Estelle "Essie" Riddell. She's also the last of the family still around to recall growing up in jail with the state's longest-serving sheriff.

First elected in 1939, Sheriff Riddell served for just over thirty-nine years, his job ending in 1978 when he died in office. He held the record as the longest-serving sheriff until 2008. A farmer, rancher, cattle driver and rodeo cowboy, Riddell and his wife had their first three children in Spicewood in southern Burnet County. The family moved to Shovel Mountain, about thirteen miles away, when Vonnie was two years old. The three sisters—Vonnie, Modena (Curington) and Daisybel (Grigsby)—each had a horse on the farm. Their grandparents ran the Shovel Mountain store, which was about a quarter mile from their house. They attended Shovel Mountain School through the sixth grade. Their aunt Grace Herbert taught there.

"Every year, the community would get together to see whose car they were going to use to drive the older kids over to the Marble Falls school," Vonnie said. At the time, her father had a truck, which he used to haul cattle to market for nearby ranchers. "That's when the Fort Worth Stockyards opened up, and we were their first customers."

Burnet County Sheriff Calvin Boyd greets Vonnie Riddell Fox in the Old Burnet County Jail Museum. Fox grew up in the jail. *Suzanne Freeman.*

At the urging of friends, Riddell ran for sheriff, winning on the first count by only twelve votes. A recount narrowed the margin to six votes, but he was in for the long haul, quickly moving his family to Burnet.

"I was scared," Vonnie said when asked about moving from the seclusion of a farmhouse surrounded by family to the Burnet County Jail. "After about two weeks, I settled in, and everything was just fine. I was happy there."

She credits her mother for making the jail a home and the friendly folks in Burnet for the welcome they gave the new sheriff's family.

As matron of the jail, her mother cooked for both the family and the prisoners. "We ate what they ate," Vonnie said. That was usually a meal of beans, cabbage, potatoes and beef. "It was good home cooking, just everyday food, whatever Mama cooked."

During the holidays, Mrs. Riddell roasted enough turkey and prepared enough dressing for everyone.

On Vonnie's most memorable holiday, her mother started having pains on Christmas Day and was whisked off to the hospital until the next evening. "We got a baby brother that night," she recalled. "We were all happy about that. We didn't have any boys in the family."

She and her sisters hurried home from school every day to help take care of little Wallace Patten Riddell. "We were three grown girls and a baby," she said. "That was something."

Vonnie loved her life on the Burnet Courthouse square, quickly adapting from the seclusion of the country to living in the center of town. School was only three blocks away, close enough that she came home for lunch every day.

The family attended the Church of Christ, which was just across the street from the jail, as was the courthouse, where her father kept an office. Two theaters on the square provided entertainment for twenty-five cents a show.

Their large family kitchen had a table that sat sixteen and was often fully occupied by family and friends. The kids would take tin plates of food to the prisoners in their cells and then sit down at the family table to eat together almost every meal.

One not-so-fond memory is of when the sheriff took Vonnie to a crime scene. A twenty-two-year-old had shot and killed his father on the east side of town. Riddell took his school-age daughter on the call to show her "what goes on in the world."

"Daddy had to arrest the young man, put him in the car and take us back to the jail," she said.

She noted that, for the first seventeen years in office, Sheriff Riddell worked alone. The county had no deputies until 1956. "It wasn't like it is now with so many more people," she said.

Sheriff Riddell also made sure his kids learned their manners. "I would go out with him and walk around the square, and people would come up to him to shake hands," Vonnie said. "If I didn't shake their hands and greet them politely, I'd get my pigtails pulled."

At twenty-four, Vonnie married Billy Joe Fox and moved back to a ranch, this one in the northern part of the county. Together, she and her husband developed the Delaware Springs golf course and community. Billy Joe died in 2018. She sold the family farm soon after. "I just don't need that much anymore," she said.

Vonnie still owns Fox Real Estate and continues to work as a consultant and Realtor. At ninety-eight, she keeps her mobile phone at her side to take business calls.

When the newly renovated jail opened as a visitors' center and museum in 2022, Vonnie was the guest of honor. It was her second recent visit to the jail. Burnet County Judge James Oakley brought her to see the renovations while underway.

"When she first walked in the door, she looked over to the side, in that corner, and I asked her, 'What are you looking for?'" Oakley said. "She was looking for the board they put across the door to barricade it. It was always leaning in that corner when she walked in."

Now, when visitors walk in that same door, they will see a replica of the board in the corner.

Built in 1884, the jail housed prisoners and a sheriff's family for much of one hundred years. In 1984, a new jail and sheriff's office built on Texas 29 opened and still houses prisoners and law enforcement offices.

When the old jail closed in 1982, probation officers moved into the limestone building at the corner of S. Pierce and Washington Streets. Interior walls were covered with chicken wire and stucco, and new restrooms were added. More than thirty-five years later, workers uncovered the rock walls and found a plastered-over listening portal on the third floor that was used to spy on inmates in their second-floor jail cells.

"We didn't know that listening port was there," Oakley said. "Someone can be in there and whispering and you can hear it clearly in here."

The steel portal is about the size of a small fist and embedded in the wall. On the other side, it is hidden from view by a grate.

All the jail cell doors were restored to working order, including one concave steel entryway that was brought from a display at the Fort Croghan Museum and reinstalled. Bars that covered one of the windows were found in a precinct barn gathering dust. They fit right back into the space and were welded into place.

The jail has two kitchens: the original kitchen, which had a locked, steel pass-through to feed prisoners in the downstairs cell, and a more modern one that was installed years later. The newer kitchen was upgraded for use during events.

Wall sconces and bedside lamps feature bulbs that replicate the look of flickering candles. No curtains block the windows, making the inside space visible from the outside, especially after hours. "I want to have it all lit inside at night so you can see the glow," Oakley said.

It looks like home to Vonnie Fox.

"I've never lived out of the county," she said. "I've always lived with Burnet County people, and I've always been friends with Burnet County people. It's like family, really. Everybody always helps each other. I've had a good life. We were happy."

Chapter 3

THE JUDGE AND JOHNNY RINGO

He was a soldier, journalist, Boy Scout leader, lawyer, mayor, county judge, district judge, Lower Colorado River Authority board member, state representative, district judge of the Thirty-Third District Court and keeper of history, especially when it came to Old West desperados. Judge Thomas Ferguson (September 3, 1906–February 10, 1991) especially enjoyed researching cattle rustler and gunslinger Johnny Ringo, whose infamy followed him from the Hoodoo Wars in Mason County to the Burnet County Jail to the mean streets of Tombstone, Arizona.

Ferguson's research files now reside in the Fort Croghan Grounds and Museum at 703 Buchanan Drive in Burnet, the site of the original Fort Croghan. The fort was one of four established by the United States Army in 1849 to protect settlers moving west. Ferguson bought and donated the land and building for the museum.

"He was a historian," said Joy Taylor, a longtime member and former Burnet County Heritage Society president. She researched and wrote the background document for Ferguson's commemorative tile in the Plaza of Honor at Fort Croghan. She was also a personal friend.

"He was so interested in the history of the fort that he wanted a place to show the public what had gone before," Taylor said. "So he bought the building and donated it to the heritage society so we could accumulate memories of Burnet County history and share it with the public."

Left: A portrait of Johnny Ringo taken about 1880. *Public domain.*

Right: Judge Thomas Ferguson at his desk, which is now in the Fort Croghan Museum and Grounds in Burnet. *Fort Croghan Museum and Grounds.*

In the corner of a room off the main museum floor sits Ferguson's desk and a filing cabinet stuffed with his papers and research on topics as varied as deed disputes and his correspondence with President Lyndon B. Johnson, a close friend.

The file for John Peters Ringo (May 3, 1850–July 13, 1882) is thick and bound at the top with brass fasteners. It includes a timeline of murders, arrests and jailbreaks, as well as court records and letters from district clerks and other researchers. In a letter dated September 30, 1976, James M. Fitzpatrick of New York replied to a letter from Ferguson with some interesting Ringo background. (Nothing in the file reveals why Fitzpatrick knew so much about Ringo. Most likely, he was a fellow Ringo researcher with a connection to Burnet County.)

"According to my information, the association that got him [Ringo] embroiled in the Mason Co. War was not Scott Cooley but John and Moses Baird (or Beard), who were residents of Burnet town," Fitzgerald wrote.

He told of Ringo's escape from jail in Lampasas in May 1876 and how he was recaptured near Castell in Llano County. Ringer was indicted in the murder of James Cheney in Mason and released on bond in December 1877. The case was dismissed in May 1878.

"Don't know what he did with himself during the last year and a half in Texas, except that he frequented Austin's Red Light district," Fitzgerald continued. "His mother died (I think in 1878), and Ringo took to heavy drinking."

According to a timeline Ferguson put together, Ringo was in Burnet County for much of the Hoodoo War (1875–76). He left Mason County for Burnet after killing Cheney in August 1875. The murder was in revenge for the killing of Tim Williamson, his friend Cooley's adopted father, by a deputy sheriff the previous May.

By December, Cooley and Ringo were in Burnet, where they were arrested for threatening to kill Burnet County Sheriff John J. Strickland. A drunken Ringo was shooting his pistols into the sky on the Burnet County Square when arrested. Moviegoers will recognize a similar scene in the 1993 movie *Tombstone*, starring Kurt Russell, Sam Elliott and Val Kilmer. In the movie, Ringo (played by Michael Biehn) is on the main street, drunk, shooting off his pistol, when he kills the town marshal. He then dares anyone to take him on in a gunfight.

Doc Holliday (Kilmer) steps out from the shadows of a saloon to accept the challenge.

"I'm your Huckleberry*," he said, a line that has become so iconic that Kilmer used it for the title of a memoir published by Simon and Schuster in 2020.

In his letter, Fitzgerald tells Ferguson that while he knows a lot about Ringo's criminal background, he lacks personal information about the man, especially about what he was like growing up in his hometown of Greensfork, Indiana.

A look into Ringo's soul can be found in Ferguson's materials. A report written on October 28, 1875, by Major John B. Jones, commanding frontier battalion of Texas Rangers, to General William Steele, the adjutant general in Mason, describes Ringo having breakfast in a hotel in Mason after killing James Cheney in the presence of Cheney's family.

"Then George Gladden, Cooley, Ringo, and others of the party rode into town and ate their breakfast at the hotel and boasted publicly at the table of what they had done, telling those present that they had 'made beef out of Cheney' and 'if somebody did not bury him he would stink,'" Jones wrote.

Gladden was interviewed by Mason County Justice of the Peace Wilson Hey, who was then asked by Major Jones why no one had been arrested.

"His reply was, no complaint had been made against them, though he held the inquest," Major Jones continued in his memo to General Steele, which can be found in the Texas State Library, Archives Division.

One reason that Cooley, Baird, Gladden and Ringo didn't face murder charges is that the investigation ended up with the Texas Rangers, and Cooley and the Baird brothers were former Rangers.

According to an article in the *Llano News* written by the late historian Karylon Hallmark Russell (July 30, 1944–October 9, 2017), Ringo arrived in Tombstone looking to start a new life. Tombstone, in 1879, was a rich but lawless mining town with plenty of opportunities for newcomers. Ringo threw his hat in with a group called the Cowboys, who worked for the Newman Clanton ranching family.

Soon after his arrival, writes Russell, Ringo began to "mentally and physically unravel." He is linked to several drunken episodes, stagecoach robberies and murders. The Cowboys' famous feud with the Earp family began with a stagecoach robbery in 1881 that led to the shootout at the O.K. Corral. Ringo was in New Mexico at the time.

Parsing the good guys from the bad in Tombstone was difficult. Each shooting resulted in a revenge killing from one side or the other. Toward the end, the Earps were hunted by a sheriff's posse that included Ringo. No one was ever brought to trial, and the Earps and Doc Holliday all left Arizona for different states.

According to several researchers, Ringo ended up killing himself in a drunken stupor. His body was found in July 1882 in Norse's Canyon with a bullet in his head and a gun in his hand.

Ringo's story has been manipulated for entertainment purposes for decades. Aaron Spelling created a TV series, *Johnny Ringo*, that aired from 1959 to 1960. In it, Ringo is billed as an ex-gunfighter turned sheriff in a small Western town—not even in shooting distance to the truth. He is portrayed as dreamily handsome in the black-and-white footage, dressed in a leather vest, cowboy hat and shiny badge.

At least eight movies were made featuring Ringo, including *Gunfight at the O.K. Corral* (1957), *Ringo and His Gold Pistol* (1966 Spaghetti Western), *The Gunfighter* (1950), *The High Chaparral* (1969), *The Lost World* (1999) and *Wyatt Earp* (1994). His character was included in numerous TV shows, from ABC's *Tombstone Territory* to *Death Valley Days*. He was also featured in an episode of BBC's time travel serial *Doctor Who*, in the seventh serial of the third series in 1966.

In Burnet, he was portrayed by a school-aged reenactor who told a brief version of this history from inside a cell in the renovated Old Burnet County Jail. Ringo would actually have been held in a cell in the courthouse across the street. The Burnet County jail at 109 S. Pierce was not built until 1884, two years after Ringo's death in Arizona.

Ringo's life and times are obviously still of interest to many. According to Taylor, Ferguson's fascination with Ringo and other locally based outlaws stemmed from his thirteen years as the district judge for the Thirty-Third Judicial District.

"He had such a knowledge of human nature," Taylor said. "I think that's why he was such a good judge. He recognized our shortcomings as human beings."

Ferguson was known for his public speaking and lay preaching. In many ways, he was exactly the opposite of the man he spent his free time researching.

"He was a Christian man," Taylor said. "He filled the pulpit of any church that called on him. He was a member of the Burnet Christian Church, but he would fill the pulpit in Johnson City, anywhere they called for him. He also talked at I don't know how many graduations throughout the district."

It could also be from his background as a newspaperman.

Ferguson was born in Roswell, New Mexico, in 1906. He found his way to Burnet at a young age, graduating from Burnet High School in 1921. Immediately after graduation, he became owner-editor of the *Liberty Hill Index*, a weekly local newspaper. He went on to own several other papers, including the *Burnet Bulletin* from 1924 to 1926.

His interests soon turned to the courts, law and government administration. He became deputy district clerk of Burnet County in 1927 and passed the state bar in 1928. He was chairman of the Burnet County School Board from 1934 to 1941 and mayor of Burnet from 1939 to 1942. He enlisted in the U.S. Army when the nation joined World War II in 1942, serving as a master sergeant when the war ended in 1945.

After returning to his family in Burnet, he was appointed Burnet County judge. Two years later, he was appointed district judge, a position he held until 1960 through three reelections. The list of jobs, positions and honors for community service goes on as Thomas "Tommy" Ferguson became involved in the Masons, the Boy Scouts, the Kiwanis, the Lions Club, the Texas State Historical Commission, Foundation and Genealogical Society, among many other organizations.

His appointment as one of the founding members of the board of directors of the Lower Colorado River Authority (LCRA) ultimately led to his name becoming affixed to a power plant in Horseshoe Bay.

Martin McLean of Marble Falls, also a former Burnet County judge and LCRA board member, said Ferguson deserved the honor of having a major facility named after him. McLean was friends with Ferguson and followed him a generation behind in many of the same community positions.

"I always had a lot of respect for him," McLean said. "The first thing that comes to mind is that he had a fantastic memory. I really enjoyed visiting with him. He could sit down and talk to you about something that happened fifty years ago and remember every detail." A fitting attribute for someone who continues to be remembered fondly long after his death in 1991.

"He was involved in so many people's lives," Taylor said. "Lord knows how many graduation announcements, how many birthday cards, he'd get every year. People throughout the district felt like they knew him personally."

And then there's Johnny Ringo, a man who would have been Judge Ferguson's nemesis had the two men shared a time period.

"He just had a fascination for desperados, especially the ones who put a little thought into it," Taylor said. "He was interested in the ones like Johnny Ringo, who didn't have a whole lot of sense but got by with a whole lot for a long time. He very definitely had a soft spot for desperadoes, and Johnny Ringo was one of them."

Perhaps Ringo's story would have ended differently if he had been prosecuted properly in Burnet County for his crimes in the Hoodoo War and on the Burnet County Square. If only there was a Dr. Who–like time machine…

* "I'm your huckleberry" was a common saying in the 1800s and meant "I'm the one for the job." Doc Holliday says it to Johnny Ringo twice in the 1993 movie *Tombstone*, the second time right before he kills him. Historians believe Ringo killed himself. In the movie, Holliday stages the scene to look like a suicide.

Chapter 4

THE GOOD, THE BAD AND DEAD MAN'S HOLE

Fire Eaters murdered Marble Falls settler Adolph Hoppe (1820–1862) during the Civil War for refusing to break his oath to remain loyal to the United States rather than voting for secession. He was vocal about his Union sympathies, and that got him killed, according to his descendants.

"He was always spoken of in the family as a heroic character who spoke his mind and didn't back down," said Robyn Richter, Hoppe's great-great-granddaughter in Marble Falls. "The story was always pretty consistent of him speaking up to the bushwhackers/Fire Eaters and probably getting himself killed for being outspoken."

Bushwhackers, also known as Fire Eaters, were secessionist vigilantes who were believed to have killed as many as sixteen people in Burnet County during the Civil War. The bodies were disposed of in a 155-foot vertical cave about three miles south of Marble Falls known as Dead Man's Hole.

Hoppe (pronounced *Hop-e*) is one of the few individuals identified among those who ended up in the bottom of that hole. Now, 160 years later, Richter has decided to set a tombstone for him in the Cypress Mill Cemetery in Blanco County.

"That's where other family members are buried," Richter said. "My grandmother—his granddaughter—is buried in Cypress Mill. That is where his offspring settled. A lot of his descendants were in Blanco County and that area around Cypress Mill."

A historical marker erected at the site in 1998 names Hoppe, Benjamin McKeever and John Scott, Burnet County's first county judge, as three of

The historical marker next to Dead Man's Hole in Marble Falls. The hole, which goes 155 feet down into the earth, has been capped. *Suzanne Freeman.*

the seventeen mostly anonymous victims. All but McKeever were killed because of their Union sympathies. Only McKeever's body was recovered within days of his death in 1871, and only McKeever's murderers came to justice.

Men began disappearing in Burnet County after 1861, the year Texas held a referendum on secession. Burnet County voted 248 to 159 to remain in the Union. Statewide, 76 percent of voters opted to join the Confederacy, which led to tension in the divided Central Texas community. According to a family history written by another great-great-granddaughter, Becky McNamara, Hoppe became a target of the Fire Eaters when he helped one of his farmhands escape conscription into the Confederate army.

"When he immigrated, Adolph had signed an oath of allegiance to the United States to be allowed to settle in Texas, and Hoppe had been vocal in his reluctance to violate that oath," McNamara wrote. "Many German Texans opposed slavery as a contradiction to what America represented."

Hoppe and a friend, Henry Flaugher (in some records Flower), were hauling a wagon filled with cedar posts they had cut to construct a sheep stable. They were waylaid by bushwhackers who accused them of attending

Mike Brittain as Adolphe Hoppe in the Legends of the Falls historical hayride in 2022. Listening is Hoppe's great-great-granddaughter Robyn Richter. *Suzanne Freeman.*

secret Union meetings. A Texas Ranger accompanied the bushwhackers to act as judge and arrest the accused if he did not believe their protestations.

Flaugher was arrested and never seen again, although the bushwhackers said they were taking him to San Antonio to jail. Hoppe argued that he was the sole provider for his wife, small daughter and ten-year-old son. He pleaded not guilty at the impromptu trial, but according to an account by Herman Richter, who was present when Hoppe's body was pulled out of the cave, the bushwhackers sneered at him and demanded he explain why he was hanging around with Flaugher.

"I do not choose my friends by their political beliefs," he is said to have replied.

Although he was at first released, only Hoppe's horses made it home.

"It was only about twenty years ago that I learned about the other man, Mr. Flaugher, killed at the same time as Hoppe," Robyn Richter said. "His family sent an email to my mother. Their story was similar to my family's."

The Richter and the Hoppe histories are also similar, typical of the thousands of German families who settled in the Texas Hill Country. Both families emigrated (separately) from Germany and settled on adjoining land in the Double Horn community south of Marble Falls. Eventually, the families intermarried. Robyn's grandfather Herman Richter married one of Adolph Hoppe's granddaughters, Marie Giesecke, and when Robyn's father, Walter, was born, he was given Hoppe as his middle name.

"I grew up knowing the story of Dead Man's Hole," Robyn said. "It was probably one of the first family stories I learned, and it helped spark my interest in family history."

Although she grew up in Austin, where her father, Walter, was a state senator and her mother, Dorothy Jean "D.J.," a well-known community activist, Robyn has lived most of her adult life in Marble Falls on the family ranch. She is a retired Marble Falls teacher, history buff and Falls on the Colorado Museum board member.

She is not the only person with a direct connection to what happened during the war years of 1861 to 1865 who has wanted to erect a monument to its victims and its heroes. In 1939, Martha McFarlin Gray of Lometa wrote to the *San Saba News and Star* to correct a previously published story and propose a monument. According to Gray, a story by W. L. Burnham in the June 30, 1939, *Burnet Bulletin* told of six unidentified men who had searched Dead Man's Hole for bones in 1870. Burnham claimed these were the only men to ever explore the hole, at least at that point. According to Gray, her father, John McFarlin, assisted a man named Benny Gibson (also spelled Gipsin and Gipson in the same article) in retrieving remains in either 1865 or 1866.

"He [Gibson, first spelling] filled two sacks with human bones and sent them out, then was pulled out, for the heavy air, the gruesome sights, and the handling of the skeletons was so much for him that he could not speak for some time," Gray wrote. "I do not know what was done with the human bones, but one pair of small wrist bones tied together with a silk handkerchief were supposed to be the wrists of John Scott, Burnet County's first Judge, who disappeared."

Until that time, the cave was known as Burnam's Hole, as it was on the Burnam Ranch (same family as Burnham, but the two branches spelled it differently). After Gibson brought up the bags of bones, it was changed to Dead Man's Hole.

"Benny Gipson [second spelling], in going down in the bosom of the earth, not knowing what reptiles it might contain or how deep the hole was, proved himself a real hero worthy of a monument," she continued. "His act took bravery, courage, determination, and a will to work and do a thing that he knew should be done, even if it was dangerous and a gruesome sight to behold and a heart rendering thought to be in the heart of the earth and handle human bones."

The *Texas Caver* published an article in its February 1965 edition that tells a similar story.

"Benny Gibson was let down into the hole barefooted," wrote article author J.T. Meador. "Gibson filled two sacks with human bones and sent them up. When he was raised, he was wearing shoes!"

According to Meador, the shoes belonged to Adolphe Hoppe.

According to an account written by Walter Richter, his grandfather Herman Richter was part of that group. Herman was sixteen years old in 1866 when Gibson was lowered into the hole.

"Grandfather Richter said he stated there were 'thousands of bones' at the bottom, both human and otherwise," Walter Richter wrote. "In later years, my grandfather asserted the sheriff of Burnet County and a group of men explored this natural grave for murder victims. Several large sacks of bones were brought up, enough, according to a report by the sheriff, for sixteen skeletons."

Walter's written account appeared in the March 1941 issue of *Frontier Times* magazine. The information also was part of the application for a historical marker that was granted by the Texas Historical Commission and erected in 1998.

The one victim who did not end up in a bag of bones was Benjamin McKeever, who was killed in 1871 in a feud over a dog that barked at him and his horse as he rode past a family farm in Spicewood. McKeever shot at but missed the dog. Although the animal was unhurt, four family members lay in wait days later as McKeever rode past again. He was on his way home from courting a young woman living on Captain Jesse Burnam's ranch. They shot him, hid the body in a creek and later moved him to Dead Man's Hole when search parties began looking for him.

Then–Deputy Sheriff Nimrod "Dock" Miller led a search party for McKeever. Searchers found one of McKeever's boots and his pistol on the aforementioned ledge just below the opening of Dead Man's Hole. They gathered up four suspects and met back at the opening of the cave.

One of the suspects volunteered to go into the hole to look for McKeever's body. He made it only partway before demanding to be hoisted back up to the surface. The deep subterranean cave was known for its "bad air," so they next sent a lighted torch into the hole. It extinguished partway down. According to research by the University of Texas in the 1960s, the cave contains highly elevated carbon dioxide and low oxygen levels. The search party knew only that breathing past a certain point was hard.

Despite the dangers, Miller decided he had to retrieve the body so the murderers could be brought to justice. Once lowered, he tied a rope to McKeever, and members of the search party pulled them up and out one at a time. Miller passed out when he reached the surface.

According to reports, McKeever's throat had been cut so deep that his head was dangling, almost disconnected. Gunshots dotted his body and clothing. The four suspects were said to be so distraught at the sight that they confessed immediately.

Later, Miller found bloody clothing that linked the four to the murder. They were arrested and tried, but records about what happened to them are unclear. All four were found guilty in January 1873 in San Antonio. According to Burnet County records, they were hanged on January 15. Another record reports that three of them were sentenced to prison and a fourth acquitted.

Miller went on to be elected Burnet County sheriff. One day, he left on a manhunt and never returned. He was last seen in Oklahoma.

One of the victims of the Fire Eaters mentioned on the historical marker, Burnet County Judge Scott, was fleeing to Mexico after being accused of supporting the Union, even though all four of his sons fought for the Confederacy. The Fire Eaters intercepted him and his friend James McMasters before they could leave the county. Both were killed and dumped in Dead Man's Hole.

Twelve other Union sympathizers are believed to have been captured by bushwhackers and hanged directly over the opening to the cave. The Fire Eaters would cut the rope, and the body would fall into a natural grave. A live oak branch that extended over the hole is displayed in the Fort Croghan Museum and Grounds in Burnet. It, too, merits a mention on the historical marker.

For Robyn Richter, who grew up with these stories, Dead Man's Hole was never a scary place or sacred ground, as it is to some. To her, Dead Man's Hole and its stories are a sad reminder of what people are capable

The hanging branch that once spanned Dead Man's Hole now hangs in the Fort Croghan Museum and Grounds in Burnet. *Suzanne Freeman.*

of. She sometimes wonders how she might have acted if she had lived in those times.

"Would I have taken the path of those mostly German people recently arrived in Texas who had taken an oath of allegiance to the United States to oppose secession, or would I have kept my mouth shut and gone along with things to stay safe?" she wondered. "In any event, Dead Man's Hole stands as a reminder of what a terrible time it was to have a country divided."

Dead Man's Hole is located on a six-acre public park on CR 401 south of Marble Falls. Then-owner Ina Lou Roper donated the land for the park before the dedication of the historical marker in 1998, which was also when the opening was permanently sealed.

PART IV

BLACK HISTORY
IN BURNET COUNTY

Chapter 1

NEW LIFE FOR STRINGTOWN CEMETERY

The 158-year-old Stringtown Cemetery, near Oatmeal and Bertram, is finally getting the recognition it deserves. It is one of only a few known all-Black cemeteries ever established in Burnet County. The Burnet County Historical Commission is determined to unearth its stories.

In 2024, the Texas Historical Commission approved an Undertold Marker for the site and a 50/50 matching grant to trace the history of the names of the families buried there, whether they have tombstones or not. Over the next three years, the money will be used to build a fence and clear brush. The Burnet County Historical Commission, which is in charge of the project, also plans to apply for a listing as a National Historic Landmark.

The state commission designated Stringtown a Historic Texas Cemetery in 2012.

"We've been aware of this cemetery and its significance for some time," said Carlyn Hammons, the Cemetery Preservation Program specialist for the Texas Historical Commission. "A cemetery like this that's associated with the freedom colonies is extremely important. They are the only visible reminders of those settlements that are left."

The term "Freedom Colonies" is unique to Texas, although similar communities popped up in other states. It refers to areas settled by newly emancipated slaves, usually outside of larger, mostly white-populated towns. According to the Texas Freedom Colonies Project, 557 of these communities existed in Texas between 1865 and 1930.

In Stringtown, former slaves built their homes side by side (in a "string") along a dirt lane, now RM 1174. The founder, the Reverend Sam Houston, is believed to be a descendant of slaves held by General Sam Houston, the first and third president of the Republic of Texas.

Reverend Houston built a combination school/church near the cemetery plot at the end of County Road 326A, two-tenths of a mile from the settlement. His gravestone records his birth as 1824, but the day, month and location are unknown. He died on May 8, 1894, in Stringtown.

Nothing but the cemetery remains of the town, which was abandoned during the Great Depression. Many residents moved to Marble Falls, Liberty Hill, Leander and Lampasas. They did not move to nearby Bertram, which, as a sundown town, did not allow non-white people in the city limits between sunset and sunrise.

"The churches and schools closed, the people moved away," Hammons said. "The cemeteries are all that's left. I'm especially encouraged that there are people trying to restore it and keep it from being forgotten. I am hoping the Burnet [County Historical Commission] will be able to uncover some additional information to add to the historical record."

Virginia and Albert Downing own the cemetery property and have maintained it for decades. A retired couple, they are no longer physically able

Opposite: Stringtown Cemetery, as seen in early 2024, before volunteers with the Burnet County Historical Commission began clearing the area. *Burnet County Historical Commission.*

Above: The tombstone for the Reverend Sam Houston, a freedman and founder of Stringtown and the Stringtown Cemetery near Bertram. *Burnet County Historical Commission.*

to continue with upkeep. Albert is a longtime member of the Burnet County Historical Commission and supports its goals to obtain a Texas Historical Marker and form a cemetery association to handle maintenance in the future.

Stringtown Cemetery has about seventy graves, fifty of them unmarked, according to a survey taken in 1982 by the BCHC. A partial list of the marked graves was included in the commission's 2011 application for a historical cemetery designation.

Until recently, the oldest graves were believed to belong to twins Annie and Eddie Jennings, both born on January 30, 1876. Eddie died first at the age of ten months. Annie died on November 21, 1877.

Lela Goar found an even older grave as she completed the grant application. Goar is the certified local government representative on the Burnet County Historical Commission.

Richard Moreland, born on March 10, 1866, lived just twenty-five days. He died on April 4. He was the son of Sara and Sam Moreland, who came to the area from Tennessee. They had ten children, most of whom are buried in Stringtown.

The most recent grave is dated October 1, 1965, and belongs to Mellie Boyce Green, who lived in California when she died. She was born in Oatmeal, Texas, on December 31, 1888. "She let her family know that she wanted to be sent back to Texas and buried in Stringtown Cemetery because of her relationship to the people there," Goar said. "Those are the kinds of things we are trying to find out through our research."

Much more paperwork lies ahead for the Burnet County Historical Commission to achieve its goal of obtaining a state historical marker, but so does a lot of physical labor, which is where the grant money comes in.

"We've got enough people volunteering to do the research for us that we won't have to use much of the money for that," Goar said. "We have a landman in place who will finish up the deed research and a lot of people willing to help with the clearing."

Nichole and Michael Ritchie, Cottonwood Shores history buffs who recently found two lost local Texas Centennial Markers, are new members of the historical commission and active in the Stringtown Cemetery project. Nichole located a Moreland descendant, Katie Wills Campbell, who lives in Leander. Campbell said she visited the cemetery once years ago and hopes to return during an upcoming cleaning session.

"I'm the baby of the family and the only one left," Campbell said. "I don't know anything about the rest of the family, but I've been doing some research, too. I haven't found much."

A distant cousin in Temple, Arthur Moreland, also said he had no stories to tell of relatives in Stringtown.

Michael Ritchie has been instrumental in helping clear the land by organizing volunteers to carefully cut back vegetation around timeworn headstones. He and Nichole also clean headstones, just as they did in the Fuchs Cemetery in Cottonwood Shores.

"While everyone else plays video games as their hobby, ours is actually going out and doing research or going to museums," Nichole said.

"Both of us are kind of history nerds," Michael added.

The search for descendants of those buried in the Stringtown Cemetery continues. Anyone with information can email the Burnet County Historical Commission at historicalcommission@burnetcountytexas.org.

Chapter 2

MEMORIES IN BLACK AND WHITE

Burnet County ranch hand Will Fish was the first generation of his family born free. According to historian Dr. Jane Knapik of Marble Falls, he was born in 1873, but despite her years of research, she has no idea where.

Learning about Fish, where he came from and how he learned ranching has proven difficult. Recent research into the Stringtown Cemetery near Bertram showed that his father is buried there. Jackson "Jack" Fish was born a slave in Kentucky in 1833. He married Mary Mathis on November 8, 1878, in Burnet. His death certificate states he was widowed; the cause of death is listed as dementia.

No record could be found of Mary's death, although a census record from 1910, six years before Jack's death, showed her status as widowed. Obviously, both cannot be true. Fish and his sister Elvira Fish Johnson moved from Stringtown, a freedom colony near Bertram, to Marble Falls, where they lived on Avenue N until their deaths. Both are buried in the Marble Falls Cemetery.

That's about all that's in the public record. Much of what Knapik has learned about Fish is from her family members, who recall how he helped Knapik's father, Lake Victor rancher Lewis E. Alexander, learn the life skills he needed to make a living. "He was so important to my dad," Knapik said. "My dad grew up as a scrawny kid with an older father. Will Fish taught my father to be a rancher."

Because of ill health, Alexander often couldn't ride the family horse to school in Lake Victor, which meant his sister Bernice was without an

Will Fish on his bed in the yard of his sister's house on Avenue N in Marble Falls. He preferred sleeping outdoors. *Dr. Jane Knapik.*

escort. When Fish stepped in to accompany Bernice to class, someone in the community complained to the family that it was not safe for a young white girl to travel alone with a Black man. "Aunt Bern told that man, 'I feel safer with Fish than I do with you,'" Knapik said, recalling the old family story.

Everyone called him Fish. He hired himself as a ranch hand and to cook barbecue and beans for large crowds. Another Lake Victor rancher, Jim Shelby, was especially fond of Fish, according to a story told by Maurice C. Shelby in a book he wrote titled *The Lake Victor Story.*

Shelby recounted, "My Uncle Jim promised him [Fish] before he died that he would see to it that a good marker was placed on his grave."

Shelby never purchased a marker, so Knapik decided to do it in 2000. Forty years after Fish was buried in a plot owned by his sister Elmira Fish in the Marble Falls Cemetery, a marker was placed stating his name and death. He died on August 20, 1960, at the age of eighty-eight. He spent his final years at his sister's home somewhere along Avenue N between St. Frederick Baptist Church and the Marble Falls Cemetery.

"His grave wasn't marked," Knapik said. "I thought it was my responsibility to get his grave marked, so I volunteered to be on the cemetery committee, and I got it marked."

Before that, one of the city's parks and recreation department employees kept a bouquet of artificial flowers on the gravesite.

Knapik has another memory of Will Fish that she transformed into a memento. When Fish was working at her father's place and everyone gathered for a meal, he cleaned his hands in a washstand on the Alexanders' back porch. Knapik had the washstand refinished, and it now serves as a bedside table in her Marble Falls home.

Knapik doesn't remember Fish from her childhood. Her family lost the Lake Victor ranch during the Depression and moved to her mother's family ranch in Uvalde when Knapik was three. She didn't see Fish until just before his death when she visited him in Marble Falls with her father. Fish was dying of tuberculosis,

Knapik began researching the man's history as she dove into her own family's genealogy. The Knapik family's roots run deep in Texas and American soil. The Alexanders moved from Arkansas to Georgetown before settling in Burnet County.

"That line goes all the way back to Jamestown in Virginia," Knapik said, referring to the first permanent English settlement in America.

On her mother's side, her ancestor George Washington Smith served at San Jacinto in the fight for Texas's independence from Mexico, which is how she became a member of the Daughters of the Republic of Texas.

Knapik has a doctorate in education from Texas A&M University and is often referred to by friends as Dr. Jane. She worked as an educator most of her life. In retirement, the ninety-four-year-old thrives on historical research, especially when it comes to Burnet County. She has written several books, one of which, *Images of America: Marble Falls*, is available at the Falls on the Colorado Museum in Marble Falls, where she serves as a docent and board member. She is working on a book about the Old Burnet County Jail, which was renovated into a museum and visitors' center in 2022.

She has no plans to write a book about Will Fish, however, mainly because of a lack of information. The anecdotal stories found in two local history books are more about how Black people were treated in the early 1900s in Burnet, not about Fish as a person.

"But I was told that the community and the people who knew him took up for him against anything," Knapik said. "People who knew him adored him."

Most of the anecdotal information came from her late father, who often talked about Fish as a mentor he was sad to leave behind when the family moved. In Uvalde, Alexander embraced his true life's passion and became a carpenter, but he never forgot what he learned about ranching from Fish.

"My dad learned a lot from Will Fish, who was a very kind teacher."

Chapter 3

A Story of Integration

Violence erupted on the University of Mississippi campus in September 1962 after a federal court ordered the school to admit its first Black student. Just a few months earlier, in May 1962, Burnet High School handed graduating senior Betty Miller Sanders its first-ever Most Deserving Student Award. Sanders wasn't the first Black student to attend BHS, but she was one of only three who attended between 1959 and 1962, the year she graduated.

"I did not want to go, but I'm telling you, it was awesome," Sanders said. "I didn't have any problems. Nobody ever let me hear it—the N-word. I had friends and I still do have friends from high school. I'm going to lunch with one tomorrow."

From grades two through eight, Black students attended what Sanders called the Black School. After that, some students went to BHS, although most went to Austin. One of Sanders's older brothers went to Anderson High School in Austin, which is where Sanders wanted to go. "But I was a girl, so no," she said.

According to Sanders, the first Black student at BHS was a young man named Kenneth Baker. He graduated when Sanders was a sophomore, according to her recollection, although this reporter could not find any mention of him in the yearbooks for those years.

At BHS, Miller was a member of the football and basketball pep squads for three years, Future Homemakers of America for three years and Speech Club for two years.

Betty Miller at the lectern in St. Matthew's African Methodist Episcopal Church in Burnet. Her mother, Emma Miller, founded the church. *The Picayune Magazine.*

Betty Miller in the 1960 Burnet High School yearbook when she was a sophomore. *Public domain.*

During her sophomore year, she remembers a team trip to Austin for a football game. On the way home, they stopped at a two-story Mexican restaurant at the corner of 6th Street and IH 35.

"We got out, and they told the coaches that I could not go in that place with them," she said. "The coach said, 'Well, if she can't go in, we can't go in.' And we were HUNGRY!"

The restaurant took them all upstairs and served them dinner, out of sight of the main dining room.

The only time she remembers being denied something in high school because of the color of her skin was a three-day senior trip to a beach near Galveston. The hotel would not allow a Black person to stay.

"My teachers were really kind to me," she said. "They asked me how I felt about that."

With a distinctive twinkle in her eyes and a chuckle as she came to the end of this particular story, she continued, "I said, 'Well, do I have to go to school those days?' They told me no, so I said, 'Well, then I'm fine with it!'"

The seventy-eight-year-old attributes her obvious high spirits and positive attitude to her mother, Emma Miller, another community dynamo who was posthumously named a Burnet County Woman of Note in 2017. Ms. Emma, as everyone called her, was born in 1904 in Brenham. She died in 1994 in Burnet.

"My mother always told me, 'You are just smarter than anybody, and everybody loves you,'" she said. "So, I went to school thinking everybody loves me. I'm just like 'Hi!' you know, to everybody."

Sanders was the youngest of seven children. She was seven years old when her family lost their farm in Liberty Hill and moved to Burnet. Her father set up a barbecue stand in Buchanan Dam, while her mother went to work for the Donald Duncan family on their Burnet County farm.

In 1953, Ms. Emma founded St. Matthews African Methodist Episcopal Church in her home.

"There was no Black church in Burnet when we moved there," Sanders said. "Mother used to have church in the living room. She thought God wanted her to do that because she loved the Lord. She loved the Lord, she did."

The Millers had attended an AME church in Liberty Hill, so that was the denomination Ms. Emma established in Burnet.

"That's what she wanted," Sanders said. "She wanted an AME church. The name St. Matthews, that was our first bishop (S.J. Matthews)."

Known as "the church that faith built," the St. Matthews building at 508 South Hill Street was created with volunteer labor and donated building supplies. Many Black families, including the Smith, Satterfield, Maxwell and Matthews families, purchased a lot at the corner of Hill and Live Oak for their sanctuary.

According to Sanders, the property was owned by a relative named Myrtle Barton.

"Her son used to live right on this corner, and Myrtle told Mother they were going to be moving and maybe she could get the building they had for the church," Sanders said. "My mother was working for a family in Burnet name of Duncan. Donald Duncan. She told them, she said, 'I need a church.' And they helped."

They moved an army barracks off the property and built their own structure from scratch. The Sunday school class made monthly payments until it was all paid off, according to a piece written by Burnet County Historical Commission member Lela Goar when Emma Miller was named a Burnet County Woman of Note decades later.

Miller secured a loan at the bank, which ended up in her name, something that was not a problem until the congregation went back to the bank for a loan to remodel in 1977. Miller was seventy-three years old and retired. She signed the deed over to the bishop for the remodel without a second thought, Sanders said.

During the remodel, the entrance and address shifted from Live Oak to Hill Street. The church celebrated seventy years on Sunday, July 23, 2023.

"When we first started the church, it was full," said Sanders, the oldest member. "Now, there are only about nine regular members every Sunday, and we are all relatives. I told the pastor when he first came, 'The worst thing you can do in this church is make one of the members upset because they are all related!'"

Sanders attended Paul Quinn College in Waco (now in Dallas) after high school. Paul Quinn is a private, nonprofit faith-based school that teaches students to "lead, live lives that matter, love something greater than themselves, and leave places better than they found them." Sanders took this to heart.

After college, she married a military man, and they were deployed to Spain, where she went to work for the government.

She remembered visiting her home economics teacher when she returned to the United States from Spain. "She said, 'Do you not know that the FBI came to my house for you?' For me?" Sanders said. "'They were asking me all kinds of questions about you,' she said. I told her, 'I hope you told them I hadn't done anything.'"

She had given her home economics teacher as a reference for her job in Spain but never thought the FBI would get involved and do a background check.

"Oh, I'm talking about myself," Sanders said. "I wanted to talk about my mother. You know she had to come where her baby was. She came to visit me in Spain and stayed for about eight months."

This interview and story were not about her mother, however. Or at least not just about her mother. Betty Miller Sanders has her own story that deserves telling. During national unrest over civil rights, Sanders continually crossed color lines to success.

After living in Spain, she worked for Southwestern Bell for twenty years, traveling between St. Louis, Dallas and Austin. She visited her mother, who lived across the street from the Burnet church, almost weekly. She moved back to Burnet in 1991. She and her new husband, Petry Sanders, bought a home in the Cassie subdivision in Buchanan Dam, where they still live. The couple has been married for thirty-four years.

As a retiree, she continued to work, selling life insurance door to door. "I knew everybody in Lampasas, Burnet and Marble Falls," she said.

That lasted three years before she was recruited to work in the human resources department for Sears. She cut the ribbon when Sears opened a store in what was then Lakeland Mall on RR 1431 in Marble Falls (where H-E-B is now). In that job, she drove to San Antonio every day from Lake Buchanan. "THAT was a job," she said.

Now retired again and active in her church, Betty Sanders visits with friends, including those from her Burnet High School days, and helps gather materials for the Black history museum being built at St. Frederick Baptist Church in Marble Falls.

She supports LACare, a food pantry in Burnet. She also helps raise money for St. Matthews to pay its assessments to the general counsel of the AME Church nationally and maintain the building locally.

"I've been blessed," she said. "I have really been blessed."

PART V

BUILT TO REMEMBER
AND REMAIN

Chapter 1
Two Dams, One Path to Power

The story behind how Buchanan and Wirtz dams were built and named includes back-room deals and good-ol'-boy chicanery that created one of the world's largest construction companies and paved a path to presidential power for a certain Texas Hill Country politician. Both dams came to be through the political machinations of a well-connected attorney, Alvin J. Wirtz, one of the dams' namesakes.

Wirtz was a well-known name in political circles in the 1930s and 1940s. He began politics as the state senator from Seguin but was run out of town when local farmers joined forces and accused him of stealing their land for government projects. At one point, a sixty-seven-year-old farmer and former Texas Ranger marched into Wirtz's office and started shooting. One person was killed and several injured, but Wirtz was unharmed.

He resettled in Austin, where he established a law firm, but not before writing the bill that created the Lower Colorado River Authority, an entity his law firm was then hired to represent.

The first challenge Wirtz faced was to find a way to complete a half-finished dam in Burnet County. What was then called Hamilton Dam was the first of five dams that created the Highland Lakes. The construction company building the dam, represented by Wirtz, went bankrupt. Wirtz set off for Washington, D.C., to find the money needed to complete the multimillion-dollar project. In the nation's capital, he enlisted the help of a young associate he was mentoring: Lyndon B. Johnson, then the legislative secretary for Representative Richard M. Kleberg.

Initially, Buchanan Dam was named after George W. Hamilton, one of the engineers of the bankrupt construction company. When Wirtz realized he needed the help of Texas Congressman James P. "Buck" Buchanan, chairman of the House Committee on Appropriations, he used his connections to change the name to honor the man who ultimately procured the funding.

Buchanan was "touched by the gesture," wrote Robert Caro in his book *Path to Power*, the first of an uncompleted five-volume biography on President Johnson. Caro includes a full accounting of Wirtz's dealings, including redrawing Buchanan's congressional district to include Burnet County and the dam.

Under President Franklin Roosevelt, Alvin J. Wirtz served as National Youth Administration director and undersecretary of the Department of Interior. *Lower Colorado River Authority.*

By the time these political maneuverings were complete, Wirtz represented the bankrupt company in receivership and the newly appointed construction company Brown and Root. And don't forget, he represented the Lower Colorado River Authority as well—the entity formed to run the dams after completion.

Wirtz was close to President Franklin Roosevelt, who ultimately made the dam a reality at Wirtz's request. Under Roosevelt, Wirtz served as National Youth Administration director and undersecretary of the Department of Interior.

Alvin J. Wirtz died in October 1951. Two months later, the LCRA board of directors renamed Granite Shoals Dam the Alvin J. Wirtz Dam.

Chapter 2

STARCKE CONTRAST

Two dams do not a Highland Lakes chain make. Step in Max Hugo Starcke, who served as general operations manager of the Lower Colorado River Authority from its first day in business. Five years later, he stepped up to serve as the authority's second general manager, a position he held for fifteen years. Starcke (pronounced Stark-e) completed LCRA's construction program, building two more dams, including the one named after him. He extended the LCRA's electrical service to thirty-three cities and eleven rural electric cooperatives.

The LCRA was formed in 1935 as a legal, state-run entity eligible to accept federal money to complete building Buchanan and Inks Dam. It was under Starcke, who took over in 1940, that the Highland Lakes chain of lakes was completed and named. According to a history timeline on the LCRA's website, as general manager, Starcke received letters from people interested in the recreational opportunities the lakes offered. He worked with state and federal agencies on the marketing plan that crowned the Colorado River chain the Highland Lakes as a promotional device. Starcke is also credited with developing the public power program that still provides the electricity that runs most of Central Texas.

When Max Hugo Starcke died in 1972 at the age of eighty-eight, U.S. Representative J.J. "Jake" Pickle read his obituary into the House of Representatives minutes.

"Mr. Speaker," Representative Pickle said, formally addressing Speaker Carl Albert from the House floor in Washington, D.C., "whenever we see economic and domestic growth in a section of our country, we usually find that one of the leaders of the growth forces is a man who has been related to an electric or energy authority. In Central Texas, that leader was Mr. Max Starcke, Administrator of the Lower Colorado River Authority."

Pickle called the LCRA "the granddaddy of river authorities in Texas."

"Max Starcke proved that the various electric authorities could work together," Pickle continued. "It is a perfect example of what can be accomplished if all the electric and energy forces help each other."

Work on the dams that brought electricity to the Hill Country and created six Highland Lakes from Lake Buchanan to Lake Austin began in the 1930s with Buchanan Dam, the largest, and ended with the completion of Starcke Dam, the smallest, in 1951. Originally named the Marble Falls Dam, Starcke Dam separates Lake Marble Falls from Lake Travis.

The dam is not the only public entity bearing Starcke's name, and generating electricity was not his only interest. In 1909, he was elected to the city council in his hometown of Seguin. In 1924, he was elected mayor and served six consecutive fourteen-year terms.

His beautification efforts in the city earned him a park to mark his legacy in Seguin. Max Starcke Park covers 227 acres along the Guadalupe River. Today, it includes an eighteen-hole golf course, a wave pool, a natural fishing area, a paddling trail, a walking trail and a playscape. In addition to a baseball-softball complex, the park has tennis, basketball and volleyball courts.

His eponymous dam holds back the waters of Lake Marble Falls, which, at 591 acres, is the smallest of the Highland Lakes. The dam features ten floodgates and generates 41.4 megawatts of electricity at full capacity. It is 98.8 feet high and 859.5 feet long. It was named for Max Starcke in 1962, ten years before his death.

Max Hugo Starcke was the first general operations manager of the Lower Colorado River Authority before becoming general manager, a position he held for fifteen years. *Lower Colorado River Authority.*

Starcke was born in 1884 in what is now Zorn, just outside Seguin. He attended what is now Texas A&M University and a San Antonio business college, paying his way as a salesman for a Uvalde coal mine. He entered the world of politics in 1906 as the clerk and secretary of State Senator Joseph B. Dibrell of Seguin.

As a businessman, Starcke subdivided and developed Sandia and Orange Grove, established a funeral home and organized a bank, all in Seguin.

As mayor of Seguin, he built the city's first water filtration plant and hydroelectric power plant. What is now known as the Texas Municipal League also owes its creation to Starcke, who served as its president for several terms.

Starcke even has a particular type of rock named after him. When Silurian outcrops were found near Llano in 1966, they were officially named Starcke Limestone.

Starcke served on the Texas State Parks Board and too many other organizations and associations to list. He was an Elk, a Mason, a Lion, a Rotarian, a Son of Hermann and a deacon at the University Presbyterian Church in Austin.

"Max Starcke offered us strong leadership and fair leadership," Pickle said as he concluded his remarks on the House floor in 1972. "We owe him more thanks than we can say for the good he did in his lifetime."

Chapter 3

INKS PENNED ON DAM, LAKE, BRIDGE

A nother name crucial to the development of the Highland Lakes is Roy Banford Inks, who, it can be said, gave his life for the endeavor. A lake, a dam, a bridge and a state park all bear the Inks name.

The progenitor of a storied Llano County family, Roy Inks died on August 4, 1935, the day before his forty-sixth birthday. His death from appendicitis and pneumonia came within days of returning home from Washington, D.C., where he was part of the Texas delegation of officials that procured the funding to restart—and finish—construction of Buchanan Dam. Inks was an influential businessman, three-time Llano mayor and member of the first board of directors for the Lower Colorado River Authority.

A Llano merchant, Inks was among the many locals who felt the economic pinch when the company building the dam went bankrupt during the heart of the Depression. Construction workers who had moved their families into the area, creating an economic boon, were now starving with nowhere to go and no means to get there. With no customers, Llano merchants were suffering, too.

Matters worsened after President Roosevelt shut down the nation's banking system on March 6, 1933. The bank where Inks kept his money, the National Bank of Llano, went into receivership and never reopened. His bank accounts, which included his Ford dealership and the store where he sold Stromberg Carlson radios and Kelvinator refrigerators, were frozen along with just about everyone else's.

Inks set his sights on getting that dam back on track.

The Roy Banford Inks Bridge in Llano County. *The Picayune Magazine.*

It took more than a year of trips back and forth to Austin and eventually to Washington, D.C., where Texas Congressman James P. "Buck" Buchanan, chairman of the House Committee on Appropriations, saw to it that the dam money came through. It took redrawing Buchanan's congressional district to include the dam and renaming it for him.

Inks left for what would be his last trip to D.C. in July 1935. According to his obituary in the *Llano News*, he was sick when he returned on Sunday, July 28, but refused to admit it. He worked until Wednesday when he was taken to a hospital in San Antonio and had his appendix removed. Also sick with pneumonia, he never recovered from the operation and died the week after his return from D.C. on Sunday, August 4.

Thanks to the endeavors of Inks and the others on the lobbying trips to Austin and D.C., construction on Buchanan Dam resumed, as did work on the dam that now bears Inks' name. Inks Dam was completed in 1938. Buchanan Dam was also completed that year.

Inks Dam separates Lake Buchanan from the Colorado River arm of Lake LBJ, forming Inks Lake. Inks Lake State Park takes up most of the land on the east side of the constant-level lake. (Unlike the LCRA's reservoirs, Lakes Buchanan and Travis, run-of-the-river or constant-level lakes maintain a more consistent water level.)

The Roy Inks Bridge crosses the other river that feeds into Lake LBJ, the Llano River. It is part of Texas 16, where it crosses the water into downtown Llano.

Originally known as the Llano Bridge, it washed out in June 1935, two months before Inks died. That flood spurred the LCRA delegation, which included Inks, to Washington for a final push for money. When its replacement was completed in September 1936, it bore Inks' name.

As interesting as all these facts are about Roy B. Inks, none of them captures the essence of the man who created the first fire department in the area, converted one of his Model Ts into the first local ambulance, introduced the first moving pictures at the original opera house and, as mayor, began the city's first street paving program.

An obvious innovator, he had a talent for marketing, driving one of his showroom autos up Enchanted Rock to prove the strength of the new transmissions Ford Motor Company was building. To prove that "even women" could drive this new car, he put his twelve-year-old daughter, Mildred, behind the wheel and had her drive through town.

Inks was born in Hoover's Valley in Burnet County but moved to Llano as a child to live with an aunt and uncle. He began his career as a traveling salesman selling seeds. He moved on to selling groceries wholesale before joining the army during World War I.

After the war, he returned to Llano, where he married Myrtle Moss, whose ancestors are embedded in Llano County history. Myrtle's grandfather Matthew Moss received 4,600 acres of land after fighting under General Sam Houston in the Battle of San Jacinto on April 21, 1836. Much of that land is still being ranched by Moss descendants.

Their two children have success stories of their own. Daughter Mildred Inks Dalrymple was awarded a Congressional Gold Medal in 2010 for her service as a Women Air Force Service pilot during World War II. She was a second lieutenant.

Her younger brother, Jim Moss Inks, was a B-23 navigator during the Second World War. He was shot down over German-occupied Yugoslavia, evading capture for eleven months. He joined the "Chetniks" resistance fighters and kept a diary of his experience.

Those notes turned into a book, *Eight Bailed Out*, which became a bestseller and a Book of the Month Club selection in 1954. He also flew combat missions in the Korean War, receiving twenty-one medals. After retiring from the Air Force, he returned to Llano, where he took over the family ranch and went into the ranch real estate business.

Jim Inks and his wife, Elsie Cloud Young, had two children who still live in the Llano area. Roy Banford Inks II, seventy-four, and his wife, Petey, live on the Inks Ranch, which his two children oversee. Roy Inks II served in the U.S. Navy before working for the Texas Parks and Wildlife Department, where he spent thirty years as a contracting specialist. Two of the parks he was in charge of were Inks Lake State Park and Enchanted Rock, which at one time was part of the Moss Ranch on his grandmother's side of the family. In fact, the Inks Ranch was the Moss Ranch until 1966. Inks II worked the ranch for sixteen years. In 2014, he suffered a spinal injury that left him an incomplete quadriplegic.

"Everybody thinks Inks is where the heritage is," Inks II said. "They came over from Hoover Valley sometime after the Civil War [1861–65]. We were here in Llano in 1857 as the Mosses. The Moss heritage is the land. The Inks heritage is from my grandpa, the shaker and mover who got into public service."

His grandpa, is, of course, Roy Banford Inks, who helped his city through the Great Depression by bringing back jobs to the Hill Country at the cost of his own health.

PART VI

FOND MEMORIES

Chapter 1

Fast Times at Old Granite School

Keeping the Old Granite School on Broadway in Marble Falls stable and functioning, whether for classrooms, administration offices or as a museum, has been a labor of love—and imagination—in this Highland Lakes community for 133 years.

It began as Marble Falls Alliance University in 1891, charging $2.00 a month for elementary students, $2.50 for intermediate and $3.00 for high school. Students could also study business or music for $4.00 or $3.50 a month, respectively. The school is built of pink granite quarried from nearby Granite Mountain, the same rock used to build the state capitol.

It became the only school building in the Marble Falls Independent School District when the district purchased the property in 1908. It served first through eleventh grade, then considered the senior year.

In its thirteen decades, it has been renovated, stabilized and reimagined multiple times, including its current incarnation as the Falls on the Colorado Museum at 2001 Broadway in Marble Falls.

Love for the building has grown as the structure ages, although talk began to stir in the 1970s that it might be time to tear it down. Then Superintendent Charles Hundley, with a sincere passion for and multiple degrees in history, stepped in to preserve what he viewed as a vital community touchstone. Hundley ran the district from 1973 to 1981. He convinced the school board to save the building, but where there was heart, there was no money.

Hundley organized a fundraiser to sell showers in the high school fieldhouse to motorcyclists blasting through town on a Labor Day ride. "Some schools

Students at Marble Falls High School in 1909. The granite building is now the home of Falls on the Colorado Museum. *Falls on the Colorado Museum.*

have bake sales," Hundley said with a smile. "We worked all weekend. I was sitting there in front of the field house in my lawn chair at a little table, and for one dollar, they could take a shower. Six hundred showers later, we had a start on the money."

Volunteers also sold tiny bars of soap donated by a local hotel for twenty-five cents each.

"That's a priceless memory," said Hundley, who has since retired in Marble Falls after a thirty-eight-year career in superintendency that included stints in San Marcos and Abilene.

The fundraiser proceeds were a drop in the bucket of what was needed. The district eventually spent $100,000 renovating the building, which was completed in 1982, two years after the Texas Historical Commission granted it a historical marker and one year after Hundley moved on to San Marcos ISD.

The memories of longtime locals go even further back than Hundley's to when the building was the only public school in town.

The fire escape on the back side of the building is an especially fond memory for four classmates who attended the school in the early 1950s. Gail Wood,

The first Marble Falls High School when its tower was still intact. The Old Granite School started as a private school. *Falls on the Colorado Museum.*

Nona Barnett Fox, Sam Burnam and Russ Roper all gathered at the Falls on the Colorado Museum recently to talk about those days. They were joined by museum board member Darlene Oostermeyer, who was not a student but spent plenty of summers climbing up the fire escape from the outside.

As an eighth grader at the school, Fox remembers a student who figured out that everyone would have to evacuate if he surreptitiously threw the fire alarm. Those on the second floor got to exit by slide.

"They figured out who was doing it, and that got stopped," Fox said. "But even after that stopped, they had to test it twice a year, so we still got to slide. We loved going down that slide."

Some enterprising students on the playground crawled up to the top to slide down during recess. That, too, was frowned upon by authorities.

"During recess and lunch, a teacher was usually standing at the end of the fire escape so we couldn't crawl up it," Fox said.

During the summer, with nary a teacher in sight, Oostermeyer made two or three runs down the slide, sitting on wax paper she pilfered from her grandmother's kitchen to prepare for hours of entertainment. "After once or twice with wax paper, you just went zipping down it," she said.

Wood, who came to school via bus from Spicewood, said he climbed up the fire escape for a quick slide any chance he got, no matter the consequences. "That always got us into a lot of trouble," Wood said. "I lost count of how many paddlings I got. Most of those were for chewing gum, though."

Burnam claims he was never paddled, though he once came close. Trouble on the fire escape saved his backside. "I was sent to the office at the same time [another student] was sent for pestering a girl upstairs," Burnam said. "Instead, he went down the fire escape so he wouldn't get paddled. I'm not sure he ever came back."

Burnam was facing punishment for pulling a girl's hair. He still has a scar on his wrist from where she stabbed him with her pencil in retaliation. "After [that student] went down the fire escape, the principal forgot all about me," Burnam said with a smile.

Another favorite memory shared between these classmates happened during a flood when students and teachers had to spend the night at the school. "Fort Hood sent helicopters to drop food to us," Burnam said. "We were so excited."

He recalled one father who swam across the creek three times to get each of his three children home.

The grade levels taught at the Marble Falls school changed as the district built new campuses. Following the 1980 renovation, the administration offices and kindergarten took over.

The late State Senator Walter Richter, who graduated in 1934 from the school his father also attended, was on hand for the grand reopening of the building in 1982. His daughter, Robyn Richter, who now lives on the family ranch south of Marble Falls, was teaching in the district at the time of his speech, although not in that building. She is now on the board of the Falls on the Colorado Museum, which is housed in the Old Granite School.

"I'm a newcomer compared to other people volunteering here," Robyn Richter said of the docents and board members who keep the museum thriving. "Being here has let me focus on this love of place that I have. It's a place I can focus my love of this area."

In his speech forty years ago, Senator Richter called the Old Granite School "the queenship of the Marble Falls academic fleet." He noted the difference in two essential functions the newly renovated building was about to take on.

"One is the administrative arm of the entire school system," he said. "The second, on the other end of the spectrum in a sense, is the kindergarten—

that program dedicated to the beginning of our children's formal educational experience. The Alpha and the Omega, so to speak!"

He emphasized the importance of "looking to where we've been" when promoting the future.

"Fifty-nine years ago in 1923, when I entered the first grade, a tow-headed tyke who spoke German and virtually no English, all grades were housed in this building," he said in his speech. "There was no gymnasium, no auditorium, no cafeteria, no vocational ag shop or courses, and no turf on the football field, only granite gravel and sandburs. Matter of fact, abrasions on legs and elbows of the gridders were badges of honor and symbols of macho, although we weren't familiar with the term in those days."

The last classroom moved out in 1987; the administration stayed until 2009, when the superintendent's office took over the former Colt Elementary School, and Colt students moved to a new building near the high school on Manzano Mile.

The Falls on the Colorado Museum leased the building from the district in 2010, adding improvements to the grounds, the buildings and the contents over the last twenty-four years. The second floor, however, was deemed unsafe for public use.

In 2024, the school board dedicated $250,000 to shore up the second floor, which the Falls on the Colorado Board of Directors agreed to match and then some. They are raising money through donations to repair the stairs and replace the windows on both floors, returning the second-floor windows to their original design. The original oak boards of the upstairs flooring have been uncovered and restored. The pressed tin ceiling, the walls and some of the blackboards have also been restored.

Another former student from the 1950s, Mary Clark Wimberly, recently visited the museum with her niece (this writer) to check out the current renovations. Wimberly's sister, Frances Naomi Clark (this writer's mother), and brother, Lloyd Angus Clark, all grew up on Broadway, just a few blocks east of the school. Their mother (this writer's grandmother), Icia Mae Wheeler Clark, attended the school as a first and second grader in 1922 and 1923.

Like her classmates, Wimberly also relished any chance to slide down the fire escape as a kid. "It was either really hot or really cold, and it got your pants all dirty and rusty," she said. "If you had on a dress, you just scooped it under you."

Mary and Lloyd were born in the house on Broadway that still stands across the road from the Marble Falls Housing Authority office between

Avenues N and J. Older sister Frances was three when they moved there. The family lived in a tent until the first two rooms of the house—the kitchen and a bedroom—were built.

The three Clark children all attended the granite school down the road. Frances recalled a favorite teacher, Mrs. Ramsdell. "She walked to school every morning with a freshly starched white shirt and a colorful skirt," Frances said. "And she always wore a flower. I thought she was the most perfect person."

Another reason she liked her second-grade teacher was that Mrs. Ramsdell caught Mary sticking her tongue out and made her hold it that way in front of a mirror for punishment. (Mary doesn't recall.) "I remember it because I thought it was funny," Frances said with a laugh.

Mary is the only one of the three siblings still around to talk about her memories, which she says drives home the importance of keeping the old building in shape and open to the public.

"I think it's very important to preserve our past," she said. "And especially that old school. So many of us went to school there. So many of us, and a lot of us are still here. It shows how much Marble Falls cherishes history."

Chapter 2

POLITICIAN OF CONVENIENCE

M artin McLean will tell you he's a farm boy and was never really interested in politics. Gladys McLean, his wife of sixty-four years, has a slightly different take on life with the now eighty-eight-year-old Marble Falls resident who served as a municipal judge, justice of the peace, county judge, school board trustee and president, chamber president and Lower Colorado River Authority board member. In fact, she takes it back even further.

"You were student body president in high school," Gladys reminds him. "And when we moved to Dallas, you were elected to a position in the Sheet Metal Workers union."

Now retired, he sits under his carport puffing on his ubiquitous cigars, remembering Marble Falls as "small-town America."

"When I moved here, there was not a single red light in Marble Falls," he said. "The only pavement was Highway 281 and part of Main Street. The roads to Granite Shoals and Smithwick were gravel roads."

As a young man in the mid-1950s, McLean lived on his family farm in Okalla, northeastern Burnet County, where he graduated from high school in Lampasas. Four years of drought brought the family to Marble Falls looking for work.

Martin hired on at the Mathes Company, a fan and air-conditioning manufacturing plant on the banks of a brand-new lake. His father got a job at Pure Stone of Marble Falls, which processed limestone at its plant on Avenue N. The plant is still in operation under a different company.

MARTIN McLEAN

JUSTICE OF THE PEACE
PRECINCT NO. 4

—DEMOCRATIC PRIMARY MAY 6TH—

(Pol. Adv. Paid for By Martin McLean, Marble Falls, Tx.)

Left: A campaign poster for Martin McLean when he ran for justice of the peace. He later served as Burnet County judge. *Martin and Gladys McLean.*

Below: Martin McLean in the board room of the Lower Colorado River Authority, where he was on the board of directors. The picture is of his first grandson. *Martin and Gladys McLean.*

His two younger brothers went to school in the Old Granite School where Falls on the Colorado Museum now resides.

Martin met Gladys at Mustang Tavern, about seven miles south of the river on U.S. 281. "It was a Sunday afternoon, and hardly anyone was there," Martin said. "Gladys's mother and I worked together at the Mathes plant and had gotten to be good friends before I even knew she had a daughter."

Gladys lived on a farm in Cypress Mill just outside Johnson City, land she still owns and has bequeathed to their three children, Kevin, Brenda Belk and Scott.

Martin began hitching a ride to Mustang Tavern every Wednesday to use their phone to call Gladys and set up a weekend date. Mustang Tavern was a local exchange for Johnson City. "It cost money to make a long-distance phone call, and we didn't have any money," Martin said.

After three years of weekend dates, the couple married in Johnson City and moved into the Darragh House, now home to My Texas Home Broker. Owner Rosa Darragh, believed to still haunt the house, was renting out rooms in the home built for her after her husband died. The Darraghs owned Granite Mountain and used free granite pieces left in a pile near the quarry's entrance to build the house.

Not long after, Republic-Transcon Industries bought Mathes and closed the Marble Falls plant. The McLeans followed work up to Dallas, living in Euless for the next three years.

As a young union leader, Martin was invited to meet President John F. Kennedy at a luncheon on November 22, 1963, at the Trade Mart in Dallas. The luncheon invitation said the event would start at noon.

"[President Kennedy] was supposed to be there at 12:30," Martin said. "He was going to come through this door over to my right, and if I was lucky, I would get to shake hands with him, but he never got there."

Martin heard the news that the president had been shot from the radio of a police officer standing next to him. "I heard it at the same time all the police officers heard it," he said.

Martin and Gladys missed the Hill Country and wanted to move back but couldn't decide between Johnson City or Marble Falls. Following the advice of Curtis Mathes, former owner of the Mathes plant and a good friend, they bought Highway Food and Ice and renamed it McLean's Food and Ice in 1965.

"Curtis said traffic was really going to pick up on 281," Martin said. "He said it would be a good idea to have a business there."

He wasn't kidding.

The McLeans ran the store, which for some years was also the Greyhound Bus Station, for twenty-six years. Birdie's Market and Home Decor now operates out of the prime location, right next door to the Blue Bonnet Cafe.

Clayton Nolan, who was mayor of Marble Falls and a Realtor, helped them sell their first home in the city and buy the one on Avenue E, where they've lived for fifty-four years. Nolan then asked for a favor.

"He said, 'I need a municipal court judge in Marble Falls, and I want that to be you,'" Martin recalled. "I said, 'I don't want that to be me.'"

Martin finally agreed to hold the position until Nolan could find someone else. Twenty years later, Martin was both a municipal court judge and justice of the peace.

Martin made history in his municipal court role, holding the state's first Blue Law jury trial. When he didn't have enough jurors to start the trial, he sent a deputy sheriff across the street to the Blue Bonnet Cafe to round up a few more people.

Testimony lasted most of the day, but the jury took only five minutes to render a verdict of not guilty against Lakeland Mall owner Bill Bray. (Lakeland Mall was where the H-E-B is now on RR 1431.) Bray had been charged with selling the same banned item—men's socks—on a consecutive Saturday and Sunday.

"The foreman said it took them so long because they had trouble deciding on who the foreman would be," Martin said. "Once they had a foreman, it was just a matter of a few more minutes."

A lifelong Democrat, Martin was appointed to the Lower Colorado River Authority board of directors by Republican Governor Bill Clements. He served six years on the board. Three years after stepping down from LCRA, he was elected Burnet County judge, a position he held for twelve years.

"Again, I really didn't want to do that," Martin said. "I really never thought about being a politician. I was a farm boy, but eventually, I decided to give it a try."

A group of Marble Falls residents urged him to run for county judge during a battle between the north and south ends of the county over where to locate a new hospital. The decision rested in the hands of the Burnet County Commissioners Court. Then–County Judge Chester Kincheloe lived in Burnet and broke a tie vote to make Burnet the hospital home.

"People down here [south Burnet County] did not like that pretty big time," Martin said.

Martin ran against Kincheloe the next time the seat was up and won by only fifty votes. It was still many years before a hospital was built in the county's southern half.

While Gladys "held down the fort and ran the store," she said, she also volunteered in the community. In fact, both McLeans have worked for years for the Helping Center food pantry, right up until the pandemic sent them home in 2020. "We've been associated with the Helping Center since 1987, which was its first year of existence," Gladys said.

They were also instrumental in setting up Bluebonnet Trails Community Services, a mental health facility.

As for the farm boy claim, it's hard to say that of someone who can say this: "I've run for election fourteen times and I won all of them."

Then again, "politician" doesn't really seem to fit either.

Chapter 3

1950 Census Taker Recounts History

With paper and pencil in hand, Vashti Tucker knocked on doors in Marble Falls, asking for the names and the number of people living in each residence as of April 1, 1950. As of 2024, Tucker, ninety-five, was living in the Lake Marble Falls neighborhood of Los Escondidos recalling fondly her days as a census taker during a time when the population of the entire county was 10,333. (It is estimated at 55,415 in 2024.)

"I had just gotten married, was out of university and had nothing to do," Tucker said. "The census came along, and I said I guess I can do that."

A graduate of the University of Texas at Austin, she was twenty-one years old and living with her husband, Dale Tucker, in the Roper Hotel, which her parents, R.O. and Hazel Brown Smith, owned and operated.

"[The Lower Colorado River Authority was] building the dams at the time, and there was no place to live in Marble Falls, so we stayed home for a while," said Tucker, who grew up in the hotel.

Her grandfather Willis Smith purchased the property from George C. and Elizabeth Roper in 1926. The Ropers built the hotel in 1888. Tucker's father inherited it when Willis died in 1940. The Smiths owned it until 1963. The building still stands now as home to several health and beauty businesses.

"It was busy and cozy," Tucker continued. "I loved the hotel, living down there on the highway. People were always coming in for this or that."

Many of her memories of what she calls "old-time Marble Falls" were stirred by the forced downtime of COVID-19 restrictions in 2020 and 2021.

Above: Vashti Tucker worked the popcorn machine at the Uptown Theater in Marble Falls, which her father, R.O. Smith, built and opened in 1942. *Vashti Tucker.*

Right: Vashti Tucker holds a photo taken of her working the popcorn counter at the Uptown Theater in Marble Falls. *Vashti Tucker.*

Homebound due to the pandemic, she began remodeling her home and going through boxes of old pictures.

"Old-time Marble Falls did not have that many people," she said. "Most lived out on ranches. They just came into town on Saturday. I guess that was why living in the hotel was so much fun. We had some real characters stay there."

One such local character came most Saturday nights, climbing into a box of linens to sleep—with his boots on.

"Mom always said, 'I wish he'd take a room so he'd only mess up one pair of sheets,'" Tucker said.

Her father also built the Uptown Theater, where Tucker worked operating the popcorn machine throughout her childhood. He named the theater after a similar operation in San Antonio, where the family briefly lived.

Tucker was born in 1928 in San Angelo, where her family ran a Mobil gas station. When the Great Depression hit, they left, moving seven times in ten years before settling in Marble Falls, where Smith served three terms as mayor.

The city was on the cusp of doubling in size when the Smiths bought the Roper Hotel. Tucker was eleven years old, and the population of Marble Falls was 1,021, according to the 1940 census. It increased by 100.4 percent to 2,046 by the time Tucker donned her walking shoes to count heads.

Growing up in the hotel, Tucker recalls suppertime when her mother would tell her to call her daddy at the theater and tell him to come home to eat.

"We had a crank phone and a town telephone operator named Ms. Birdie," Tucker said. "I'd ring, and the operator would answer. I'd tell her the number, and she'd say, 'Oh, he's not in his office. I'll call, but I know he's not there.' It was kind of like having your own secretary."

Her father's years as mayor were especially fun, she said. He spent a lot of time at the Blue Bonnet Cafe, making deals and friends.

A man from New York came to town to explore manufacturing opportunities at the old factory on the north shore of Lake Marble Falls. The concrete bones of that factory can still be seen just west of the bridge. The New Yorker got to know the family and sent the newlywed Tuckers an eight-piece silver serving set, although the factory deal fell through.

"As mayor, Dad got called for just about everything," Tucker said. "One lady called and said, 'You have to come get this cow out of Ms. So and So's yard.' So he did."

A letter he ran in the *Marble Falls Messenger* in 1955 thanked his voters for their support and listed his accomplishments: "pavements, city water works, street lights and many, many concrete culverts and graveled streets."

"It's a long, hard fight to build a town and community, and we are and have been glad to contribute our mite toward that end," he continued in a copy of the article Tucker found in her keepsakes. "I wish to take this means of thanking you for your cooperation and support as Mayor for the past eight years. You have been swell, and I appreciate it very much."

Smith died five years later, in 1960, of Parkinson's disease.

Although working the popcorn stand at the Uptown was Tucker's first job, she was not paid for that gig since it was a family operation. She earned her first paycheck as a census taker, although she doesn't recall how much she made. Her salary was certainly not the sixteen to twenty dollars an hour offered for the 2020 census. On January 25, 1950, Congress raised the minimum wage to seventy-five cents an hour from forty cents, so her pay was probably closer to that.

Tucker went door to door with a big notebook, asking each household the same questions: Who lives here? How many children? What is your wife's name?

"The most important thing, we were told, was to write it all down as neatly as possible," she said. "You're doing this all by hand, and we had to write legibly. Your work was judged by how hard it was to read your writing."

What she remembers most about the job was dealing with dogs.

"I learned to watch out for the little dogs," she said. "They are meaner than the devil. They just want to get at you. That's when I first became afraid of little dogs. They just bark and bark."

Tucker was pregnant with the first of their three children as she counted the 2,046 people recorded as living in Marble Falls then. After a year at the Roper, she and Dale bought a home they had to move to the end of Second Street on the east side of U.S. 281 when the Wirtz and Starcke Dams were built. It would have been underwater if they hadn't moved it. It was torn down in 2020.

"It was the only house down there, and it was really nice, but the sun beat in on an afternoon," she said. "I told Dale, let's go across the river so we don't have the sun on us." That marked their first foray into Los Escondidos on the shadier south side of the newly formed lake.

In 1963, Dale took a job with the Lower Colorado River Authority and moved the family to Austin, or as Vashti puts it: "he drug us down there until he retired."

A 1945 graduate of Burnet High School, Dale began his career as a concrete inspector on the Max Starcke Dam, which separates Lake Marble Falls from Lake Travis. Armed with an electrical engineering degree from

UT Austin, he worked his way to executive director of the electrical division over his forty years with the authority. They had been married sixty-five years when he died in 2015.

Tucker still lives in the home she and her husband built on their Los Escondidos property near the dam. She was a homemaker most of her life, except for the four months a year for seventeen years that she worked for the IRS. Throughout her time in Austin, she dreamed of returning to Marble Falls. Once back home, she became involved in the community once again.

She has long volunteered at the Chamber of Commerce Visitors Center, is a docent and board member at the Falls on the Colorado Museum and is a member of the Highland Lakes Quilt Club and the First Methodist Church of Marble Falls.

Tucker brought that same dedication to community to her job as census taker, she said.

"I had a sense of pride about my job," she said. "And it was something to do."

PART VII

MERRY MERCHANTS

Chapter 1

McGill General Store
Gone with the Wind

More than 116 years of history crumbled into a pile of rubble on March 22, 2021, when seventy-five-mile-per-hour straight-line winds laid waste to the building that once housed A.B. McGill & Company General Merchants in Bertram.

Empty since 1997, the sight of the building and its fading signs still filled the hearts of many longtime locals with fond memories of buying wedding china, church shoes, party dresses, washing machines, groceries and caskets in the place where they also banked.

"It was an amazing store inside," Burnet County Heritage Society member Judy Lively said. "The bank was the most memorable part to me. It had a teller window with a marble top and iron bars. I remember that more than anything."

One day after hurricane-force winds scattered rock from McGill's outer walls across Texas 29, bulldozers were called in to finish the job. Maynard Construction Services hauled the rock away, but not before allowing residents who wanted a memento to grab a piece.

"That was too much for me," Jim Carlile said when asked if he went to the site after the building fell. "It was too sad to see it all in pieces. I was devastated."

Carlile spent much of his life working at McGill's. He and his younger brother, Phil, now in California, lived with owners Bob and Ada Reed Brewer through their high school and college years. The brothers stayed with the Brewers after their parents moved from the area for work. Jim was sixteen and Phil fifteen, and they wanted to finish high school in Bertram.

A faded pink shopping bag and a white handkerchief with the price tag still on it that was purchased at McGill & Co. in Bertram in the late 1960s or early 1970s. *Suzanne Freeman.*

Maynard Construction Services of Burnet demolished the A.B. McGill & Co. building the day after it was destroyed by seventy-five-mile-per-hour winds on March 22, 2021. *Mark Stracke.*

Carlile continued to work weekends at the store while in college and even when he and his wife, Judy, and their three kids lived in San Antonio. He moved back to help Bob with the store full time when Ada Reed died in 1991. He and Judy now live in Burnet near a golf course where he plays almost daily. The Brewers were family, he said; the store was part of his DNA.

"I can remember the McGill smell," Carlile said. "It reminds me of a leather shop but not quite the same. You could smell the wood, the oil on the wood, the sawdust we used to soak up the oil."

Each section of the store had its own large tarp fitted to cover the displays and keep the dust at bay. The main cash register, a behemoth with keys in monetary denominations rather than single numbers, had a stack of drawers underneath—one for each employee to use exclusively. Displays sat on cabinets with drawers for even more merchandise.

"They never threw anything away," Carlile said. "They just put it in a drawer. You never knew when someone would need just that thing."

Carlile's fondest memories involve "just being with BobandAda Reed," a couple whose name is still spoken today as one word. Similarly, Ada Reed Brewer is never referred to as just Ada or Mrs. Brewer. She is Ada Reed, a community supporter who still has an impact thirty-three years after her death.

Ada Reed McGill Brewer's grandfather Archibald Brown McGill began working at the store for $100 a month when it was known as T.S. Reed and Son. Reed had moved it to Bertram from South Gabriel when the Austin and Northwestern Railroad bypassed the smaller town in 1882.

The original building was made from the stone of South Gabriel's school building, carted from one town to the other when the railroad was built through Bertram. That building served as Reed's store until son D.C. Reed had a new, bigger building constructed next door in 1905. The original building was also destroyed by the March 22 storm. When it was destroyed, it housed Bertram Blend & Boutique, a combination coffee shop and clothing store.

The McGill building at 130 West Texas 29 stood for a total of 116 years, serving in retail for 111 of those years, making it the oldest mercantile institution in Texas.

McGill bought the store from Reed in 1912, and while they were no longer partners in business, they were still brothers-in-law, having married sisters Clara (A.B.) and Laura (T.S.) Moses. Ada Reed's middle name—Reed—melded the two mercantile giants into a dynasty that continued until the store closed in 1993.

A.B. ran McGill's until his death in 1934. Wife Clara took over, with daughter Ada Reed stepping in full-time in 1939. When Clara died in 1949, Bob and Ada Reed became the final owners and operators.

"Ada Reed was the store," said Lynda Reed French (no relation), a lifelong Bertram resident. "She was always good at assisting us. We bought our cloth there for our 4-H projects, and she would help us pick out shoes and gloves and hats because we had to model our projects. She would even loan us stuff for modeling. And she always loved to know how we did, how we placed. She was always interested in everything."

French still treasures a faded pink paper bag with a black sticker that has the words "A.B. McGill & Co. YOUR FASHION ADVISOR" printed on it in white letters. Inside, she keeps a linen handkerchief she bought at McGill's for three dollars. The price tag is still attached.

"That's from the late '60s probably, maybe the early '70s," she said. "This pink used to be really bright, but it's faded over the years."

Memories of the store have not faded, however, and are as cherished as French's white linen hankie.

Mary Bruce Allen, another lifelong Bertram resident, worked at McGill's off and on for twenty-two years, starting when she was fifteen.

"It was something very unusual for a town this size to have a store of that caliber," she said. "They carried Cybis porcelain and Lalique Crystal. We had a lot of customers come just for that. They had some unique, limited pieces."

People came from all around to shop at McGill's, said Allen, who now works as a teacher's aide at Bertram Elementary School. She recalls a store stocked with just about everything you could buy, which made inventory month each January a little overwhelming.

Allen was heartbroken when she saw the building in a heap.

"That's a landmark; it's always been there," she said. "But it was also sad to see it sit there empty."

Although devastated by the storm's damage, Carlile's grief is as much centered on the demise of the business.

"It was just such an institution," he said. "I hated to see it go. It was everything to the community."

The building housed an antique store until 1997 and has been empty ever since. Before it fell, it was listed for sale on several real estate sites for $1.5 million.

For Carlile, the importance of the store goes beyond anything it had for sale within its walls or the value of the land beneath its cornerstone. He called the McGills "very generous people," remembering how they often helped the community during times of need. They bought the town's Christmas tree every year and helped bridge budget gaps at the fire department, just to name a few of their contributions.

They also put together a time capsule at some point in the store's history. It was uncovered in the rubble. The capsule, a five-hundred-pound cornerstone and a sign with Reed's name engraved on it are most likely going to the Bertram Library, said Lori Ringstaff, president of the Bertram Chamber of Commerce. She stressed that specific plans for where specific artifacts may end up have just begun. That was in 2021.

"The time capsule was opened, but it hasn't been gone through," Ringstaff said. "There are some papers and other things, but we didn't want to touch anything until someone can come and do it properly." The capsule had still not been examined in the fall of 2024.

The library will most likely be the repository for most of the artifacts, Ringstaff said.

"We want it to be somewhere where everyone can see it and have it be part of the town," she continued.

For both Allen and Carlile, a library exhibit would be a fitting tribute to the couple who helped build the town and had such a positive influence on its residents.

"I learned a lot from those two people," Allen said. "When I started there, I was a little shy, and it kind of brought me out of that. I think I have a good work ethic, and they taught me that. They were just really good people."

"Bob and Ada Reed, they made me and my brother," Carlile said. "They gave us lots of guidance, helped us make the right decisions in life. It's an honor to be part of that little bit of history."

Chapter 2

POTTS AND ATER, FOUNDERS, FARMERS, MERCHANTS

Polly Krenek wakes up every morning in the same house she grew up in as a young girl, although it certainly doesn't look the same. The home in Oatmeal where she was born has been renovated many times over the years as Krenek moved away to go to school, get married and raise children. She and her husband, Michael, moved in after her mother died in 2000.

"I was born in that house and lived there until I was eighteen," said Krenek, who returned to Bertram in 1984 after years in Houston. "I remember [my family] redoing the kitchen [the first time]. My mother was cooking on an old wooden cookstove, then she got all new appliances."

Krenek's roots run deep in the Bertram area. "I'm one of the original Potts and Ater," she said proudly. "My mother was a Potts, and my grandmother was an Ater.

For those who don't know, Potts and Ater Brothers was a mercantile store and unincorporated bank in Bertram co-owned by members of two of the first families to settle in the region. Descendants of both families still own ranches in Joppa, Mahomet and Oatmeal.

George Melvin Ater, Krenek's great-great-grandfather, moved to Central Texas around 1853. He received a land patent for 320 acres in April 1857. Nine months later, the house he built became the first post office and stagecoach stop on the Lampasas to Austin route. The Mahomet stop supplied fresh horses for the stagecoaches.

Polly Krenek tracing her family history at the Herman Brown Free Library in Burnet. *Suzanne Freeman.*

Where he got the name is no mystery. Before moving to Texas from Illinois, he lived near a community called Mahomet, home to the local post office.

The Mahomet, Texas, post office and stagecoach stop remained in Ater's home for twenty-five years. In 1882, railroad tracks connecting Lampasas and Austin bypassed Mahomet for Bertram, eleven miles away. The Bertram post office, which opened on December 8, 1882, took over mail delivery. Even George Ater began retrieving his mail from the Bertram facility.

Two of George Ater's sons joined with a couple of Potts brothers to form the Potts and Ater Brothers mercantile and bank sometime around 1916 on part of the land where the current Bertram Library now sits at 170 South Gabriel Street. It closed in 1926 after the bank went bankrupt. It was co-owned by brothers Robert B. Potts and Virgil H. Potts and brothers Levi David "Bud" Ater and Allen Jewell Ater.

Another of the brothers, Jonas Sanford Ater, was Krenek's great-grandfather.

Krenek, of course, was not born when Potts and Ater Brothers operated on Bertram's main thoroughfare. That was the time of her grandmother Gussie Mabel Ater Potts. Gussie Ater married Roy Potts Sr., a Potts and Ater union that lasted much longer than the mercantile store.

"The only memory I have is of the Harvey Potts store in Bertram," Krenek said. "He opened a grocery store there after Potts and Ater closed."

Krenek has fond memories of growing up on the family farm with her parents and three sisters. She recalls endless games of dominoes, but their dominant activities revolved around chores.

"I learned to drive a tractor when I was five," she said. "I drove a Farmall F-12 tractor. I was so short that I had to slide down in the seat to put on the brakes. Daddy said, 'Do not run over the peas!' I had to keep the two wheels between the rows of peas."

A trip to Austin was rare since it took half a day to get there. Trips to Bertram, where she and her sisters loved to visit the stores, were more frequent.

"Ottinger's Five and Dime was my favorite," she said. "I just loved Ottinger's. They had all kinds of stuff there, like material and thread and knickknacks."

She also spent time in McFarlin's Drug Store and V.H. Potts Grocery. She recalls a hotel on the main drag, the Hodges Hotel, and W.O. Witcher's Ice Station. If she wasn't related to the people who owned and operated these establishments, she knew them well as friends.

"Bertram, at one time, was a fairly large, growing town," Krenek said. "We had several gins and car dealerships here, too."

Bertram is experiencing another growth spurt as the development continues to move west from Austin along Texas 29. Meanwhile, the Kreneks still raise livestock on their family land, recently adding goats to their traditional cattle herd. They also plant a few crops to feed the animals.

The family has plans to carry on into the future as well. One of her four children is currently building a home there, while Krenek is once again remodeling that kitchen.

Chapter 3

BEFORE TIME RAN OUT
ON GRAHAM'S WATCH REPAIR

For at least four decades, a sign advertising Graham's Watch Repair hung on the Graham family home wedged between a Marble Falls school and RR 1431, drawing customers and curiosity. Positioned as it was right on the highway with the Marble Falls Elementary School in its backyard, the white clapboard house drew speculation, especially after it sat empty and dilapidated for more than a decade.

"My son and a lot of friends always thought it was haunted," one father of an elementary school student said.

The home's last occupant, Houghton Graham, was the second of three sons of Corbett and Jalina "Jay" Graham, who built the house. Houghton taught himself how to repair watches and clocks by reading books. His eidetic memory allowed him to retain everything he read and every clock he fixed for every customer.

"He was a brilliant man," said second cousin Darlene Oostermeyer, who grew up with Houghton and his brothers and cared for them in their later years. "He could pick up a clock or watch manual, and he would know exactly what to do. It was astounding to watch him work."

Customers would leave their timepieces on the porch with a signed note stating the problem. Houghton fixed them and collected cash when they came back to pick up their goods. A jeweler in Burnet brought their toughest repair jobs to Houghton, Oostermeyer said.

In 2022, the eighty-four-year-old house was torn down and the property sold to the Marble Falls Independent School District, which moved its fence and expanded the school's playing field.

Middle brother Houghton (*left*), oldest brother Dempsey, parents Corbett and Jay and youngest brother Taylor Graham in front of the only home the brothers ever knew. *Falls on the Colorado Museum.*

Workers found two vintage travel clocks in the walls and three hundred brown snuff bottles with cork tops under the house. The only items of any worth were five violins and seven stunning antique clocks, Oostermeyer said. She also salvaged an antique side table now in her home. Houghton's work desk, an unrepaired clock and some of his tools are part of an exhibit in the Falls on the Colorado Museum in Marble Falls, where Oostermeyer is on the board of directors.

The 1,100-square-foot house was home to both Graham's Watch Repair and the five-member Graham family. Along with the parents and Houghton were Dempsey, the oldest boy, and Taylor, the youngest. They all lived in the house their entire lives, the three brothers sharing a bedroom with three single beds. Dempsey and Taylor died in the house. Houghton died in a hospital after a few years in a nursing home. He was the last to go.

Work was an easy commute for them all. Corbett and two of his sons, Dempsey and Taylor, worked for the school district their entire lives as janitors and bus drivers. The back of the house opened onto the athletic field of what was first the Old Granite School (where the Falls on the Colorado museum is now housed) and later where a new Marble Falls Elementary School was built.

The house sat empty after Houghton was moved to the nursing home just a few years before he died in 2012.

Its precarious position on the shoulder of RR 1431 was not where it was initially built. Before the gravel road was paved to become a highway, the house sat just above the floodplain of the Whitman Branch of Backbone Creek. That is now the location of a 1431 bridge.

The Texas Department of Transportation moved the house from the creek and then again later, repositioning it just a bit back from the road when the highway was widened. TxDOT built the concrete stairs from the road's shoulder to the front porch, which can be seen in the only picture that exists of the entire family.

When the parents were alive and the boys were young, the house hummed with music from a large upright piano, fiddles, banjos, mandolins and guitars. Oostermeyer's father, Leslie Elbert Farmer, joined in on Saturday nights when the kids would climb on the three single beds in the brothers' bedroom and listen to the Grahams jam along with anyone else who showed up.

"We lived across the road by where the car wash is now," Oostermeyer said. "Dad and I would walk down there on a Saturday night, and they would all play. We sat on the beds on these wonderful quilts, and it was so warm. There was a huge potbelly stove in the room. Most played fiddles, but Dempsey played piano."

The piano has its own story. After the parents died, the house fell into disrepair and was red-tagged for eviction by the city. Oostermeyer organized family and community members to help get it back in shape so Houghton could live out his life there.

"They were hoarders," she said. "It was unbelievable, but when Aunt Jay was alive, the house was immaculately kept. Not by Aunt Jay. She never did a thing! Dempsey did all the cooking and cleaning."

During a major clean-up, Oostermeyer got rid of a lot of the old furniture and a giant wood-burning kitchen stove. As for the piano, when she opened the top, she found dead cats stuffed inside. She and a cousin cleaned it as much as they could but couldn't find a taker.

Word got around they were cleaning out the old place, though, and one day, she got a call from another of the cousins.

"It was his grandmother's piano," Oostermeyer said. "He does not know how it got from his grandmother's house to the Grahams' house, but he came and got it and finished cleaning it up. Now he has his grandmother's piano."

After Jay died, the house fell into disrepair and disarray. With his mother gone, Dempsey quit cleaning, Oostermeyer said.

According to a story she heard from the late Reverend Max Copeland of the First Baptist Church of Marble Falls, the Graham boys doted on their mother. One of Copeland's many visits to the Grahams was on Jay's birthday. At the time, she was in a wheelchair, having lost both legs to diabetes. Everyone in the family except Taylor suffered from the disease. Houghton lost most of his eyesight to diabetes but was able to continue his repair work thanks to watchmaker magnifying glasses.

"Brother Max said they had put a crown on her head that said 'Princess,'" Oostermeyer said. "It may have been one of her last birthdays. He told me they revered her, which I guess is why they never left the nest. They never dated, never married."

Houghton did have an almost sweetheart at one point. He confided in Oostermeyer that his biggest regret in life was not marrying the young lady, who seemed to return his affections. She ended up marrying someone else and moving to Llano.

"He said his mother wouldn't let him because he was their biggest moneymaker," Oostermeyer recalls. "He not only fixed clocks and watches, he was an extraordinary woodworker. He used to refurbish antiques, too. Everyone paid in cash."

At the end of his life, Oostermeyer learned her cousin kept a stash of cash in a box under his bed. When he could no longer travel, she came by to see if he wanted her to pay his property taxes for him. He pulled out the box and counted out enough money for her to pay the bill.

"He had several thousand dollars under that bed," she said.

During the final clean-out before the house was demolished, Oostermeyer collected the unrepaired cuckoo clock, now in the museum.

"I tried for the longest time to find the owner," she said. "Eventually, I found a cardboard box with cuckoo parts and a name on the bottom with an index card."

She tracked down the owner's daughter and asked if she wanted the clock back. The young lady asked if it was fixed.

"I said, no, it wasn't, and she said she didn't want it if it wasn't fixed," Oostermeyer said. "That's how I ended up with the clock. It had been on Houghton's desk for years."

In refinishing the desk, Oostermeyer discovered that Houghton had carved into it the names of his deceased animals, the type of animal they were and the day and time they died. The family always had a lot of animals.

"When the city red-tagged the house, animal control came by and picked up fifty-two cats," Oostermeyer said.

Houghton Graham wrote the names of the family pets that died, including the time and day, on the inside of his work desk. *Suzanne Freeman.*

Houghton was well known in the community. He taught his skills to apprentices, who carried on the trade, one in Leander and one in Smithwick. When he moved into the nursing home, he moved in among friends.

"A lot of people were there that Houghton knew," Oostermeyer said. "Cleaning out that house and making it livable for him was a labor of love. It gave him a couple of years in the only home he ever knew."

The little that Houghton Graham left behind is still close to his home and work. The museum where his desk, the cuckoo clock, photo and tools are exhibited is just steps away from where his house once stood between the highway and the school building where his father and two brothers worked.

Chapter 4

How Burnet Got Connected

A Burnet Telephone Company customer gave owner James Leslie Luther Sr. his worst chewing out sometime in the early 1960s. Luther Sr. was moving party line customers to single private lines, and at least one person didn't like it.

"This lady called him up and told him he had ruined—just ruined—everybody's social life," said Burnet native Jim Luther Jr., James's son. "Party lines were where everybody got their information back then."

That sense of community still thrives in Burnet despite the loss of phone operators who plugged and unplugged wired connections from their posts on the second floor of the historic Badger Building on the courthouse square.

As the Precinct 2 commissioner for Burnet County, Luther Jr. can see the Badger Building from the east side of the courthouse where he has an office. In 2019, he inspected a newly erected Texas Historical Commission plaque affixed to the Badger Building's limestone facade. "It mentions the telephone company right there," he said, touching the raised metal lettering. "This is the first time I'm reading this."

The building has been renovated and now houses Wedding Oak Winery, a vibrant part of downtown Burnet, which includes a bank, antique shops, restaurants, county offices, a library, several churches, Main Street Bethlehem and a museum in the Old County Jail, also recently renovated.

As a small child in the 1960s, Luther spent a lot of time on the second floor of the building at 229 South Pierce Street, where his dad often dropped him off for the operators to babysit. He recalls a growing business.

Burnet County Commissioner Precinct 1 Jim Luther next to the Badger Building Historical Marker, where his father started the area's first telephone service. *Suzanne Freeman.*

"Every time somebody would get a new line, they would cut the screen out a little bit bigger to run the line through the window," Luther said. "That hole just grew bigger and bigger."

Luther Sr. purchased the company in 1954 with business partner J.D. McDuff. The pair soon owned telephone businesses in Killeen, Copperas Cove, Crockett, Fort Hood and several other small communities. It grew so big that the company acquired a Douglas DC-3 plane similar to the military version C-47 Skytrain for transportation.

"We lived out near where the Hill Country Fellowship Church is now," said Luther, referring to the church on Burnet's south side near the municipal airport. "Dad built that house. I grew up in there. When Dad would come in, they would buzz the house with those twin engines—they were loud—and that's how we knew we had to go out and pick Dad up."

Luther's father, known as "Big Jim" Luther, died in 2018 at the age of ninety, just six months after a series of interviews with the Burnet County Historical Commission. An entrepreneur who opened one of the first car lots in Burnet, the elder Luther and his wife, Sissy, were both licensed pilots. He served on the Texas Aeronautics Commission and was instrumental in bringing Southwest Airlines to Dallas Love Field. He also helped establish Shepperd Memorial Hospital in Burnet, where Luther Jr. was born in 1963.

A 1982 graduate of Burnet High School, the younger Luther left town for college but came right back after receiving his degree from Tarleton State University in Stephenville.

"I got back home as soon as I could," he said. "This is where I wanted to be. I have never wanted to live anywhere else. I've always loved Burnet County."

Since his return, he has owned a feed store and a specialty advertising business. After years as a volunteer firefighter, he trained at the academy and was offered a job by then-Chief William DeLeon. Luther Jr. was deputy chief when he retired as a firefighter, just before being elected to the Commissioners Court in 2016.

Growing up in Burnet, he recalls a community that lived life at a slower pace than today and where residents never felt the need to lock their doors.

"I remember when you could pull up at the intersection at [U.S.] 281 and [Texas] 29—the only red light in town—and know somebody at one of the other three corners," he said.

The place to meet and greet, whether young or old, was A&O Pharmacy on the square. That's where kids would sometimes run into Sheriff Wallace Riddell, the longest-serving sheriff in Texas. "If you ran into Wallace, he would take a quarter out of his pocket and lick it real good and stick it in the center of your forehead," Luther said. "And that thing would stick! You got to keep the quarter when it fell off."

A&O Pharmacy is long gone, as is Sheriff Riddell, but their impact on Burnet and the people who call it home lives on.

"Burnet County will always have its identity," Luther said. "Forty years from now, somebody will be standing here telling someone else how good the good old days were, and they're going to be talking about what it's like right now."

Chapter 5

SNAKES ALIVE IN SPORTING GOODS

Burnham Brothers Sporting Goods put Marble Falls on the world map in the 1950s and '60s with a booming international business in predator calls and a storefront window full of live rattlesnakes.

Siblings Rhonda Burnham Lange and Bill Burnham grew up in the business, taking care of the snakes, catching minnows to sell for bait and doing any other "dirty jobs" their dad and uncle found for them. "We always got the dirtiest jobs, but they were usually the most fun," said Bill, who especially liked seining for minnows, though he could have done without cleaning the four minnow tanks every week.

The store opened in 1959, already famous for its popular coyote call. It was located on H Street across the road from Blue Bonnet Cafe and next door to where Brown's Cleaners used to be (now Double Horn Brewing Company).

"Our grandfather J. Morton Burnham discovered that coyotes would come to the sound of a rabbit in distress," Rhonda said. "Winston and Murry made plastic mouth calls with a rubber band in the middle. It sounds just like a wounded rabbit."

Rhonda and Bill's father, Winston, and his brother Murry developed a four-piece call with a reed that could be mass-produced. From there, the business took off, first as a mail-order company out of their homes.

When they moved into the store, the display window was set up to look like a campsite. Soon, they added a bullsnake, but the eight-foot-long reptile kept escaping. "It didn't matter what we put him in, he could get out," Rhonda said.

The left front window of the Burnham Brothers Sporting Goods store in Marble Falls was usually full of live snakes. *Falls on the Colorado Museum.*

Not to be deterred, the brothers came back from a Rattlesnake Roundup in Sweetwater one day with one hundred rattlers they caught. They chose the meanest ones for the new window display.

"The meaner ones were more active," Rhonda explained. "They would strike at the window. People really enjoyed watching them."

Bill and Rhonda learned to respect rather than fear the snakes, treating them with caution. Bill remembers the most excitement in the window happening when they added an alligator to the mix. "It all went pretty smoothly until a snake bit the alligator in the eye," Bill said. "The snake didn't survive that. The alligator just chomped him. Alligators are truly fast when they want to be."

For a short time, the Burnhams kept a box on the front counter labeled "Baby Rattler." Inside was a tightly wound rubber band with a paper clip on it. When you opened the lid, it released the rubber band, causing the clip to strike the sides and sound like a rattler. "We had a couple of people who got really frightened," Bill said. "We had to stop doing that, but it was so fun when you saw people's faces when they opened that box."

Only one family member did not take to the snakes: their mother, Elizabeth "Tina" Burnham. "She hated rattlesnakes, just hated them,"

Rhonda said. "She would never look in that window. If she had to walk past it, she would pull her hat down or put her hand up so she wouldn't have to see in there. That's the only thing I can think of that she was ever negative about."

Well known and respected around town in her own right, Tina was the first Head Start nurse for the Marble Falls Independent School District. During World War II, she served with the U.S. Coast Guard Women's Reserve. She attended Columbia University in New York to become a pharmacist first class SPAR. She later went to nursing school.

While everyone in town knew Tina, the hunting world was fascinated with Winston and Murry. In 1961, Hollywood star Roy Rogers asked the brothers to come out to Los Angeles to help him kill a coyote plaguing his ranch.

"I don't know about Bill, but I was ecstatic," said Rhonda, who was about ten years old at the time. "Dad brought me back [a toy] Trigger and Roy Rogers on a horse."

"I was too small to know about it," Bill said.

As Bill grew, he related more to the famous hunters drawn to his father and uncle's expertise. "They knew everybody," he said, naming Fred Bear, whose videos of hunting polar bears with a bow were popular at the time, and safari hunter Wally Taber, also known for his TV hunting shows, which were filmed in Africa.

Working together, the Burnham brothers were instrumental in getting several hunting laws on the books in Texas. They worked closely with the Texas Parks and Wildlife Department to establish an archery-only season for white-tailed deer and helped change a law prohibiting the sale of any part of a white-tailed deer. That last one was self-motivated. The brothers needed to buy antlers to make a hunting lure that could call up bucks.

"Once that law changed, we bought two thousand antlers from someone and cut them up to make rattlers," Bill said. "We cut off the tips and put a string between them," Rhonda said. "They sold like hotcakes. We all helped make them."

The Burnham family's role in Texas history predates the predator calls that made them—and Marble Falls—famous in the mid-twentieth century. Rhonda and Bill's fifth-great-grandfather Captain Jesse Burnam (spelled without the *h*) rode into Texas as part of Stephen F. Austin's original three hundred settlers in 1821. He established Burnam's Crossing, a trading post and ferry on the Colorado River in what is now Fayette County.

A historical marker at the ferry site tells of when Sam Houston and his army crossed to escape Santa Anna's forces. Houston ordered Burnam to burn the ferry and station, which included his home and store. Burnam complied.

The captain moved in 1855 to Burnet County, where he raised sheep and grew wheat. Sam Burnam (also no *h*) still ranches on that land.

More than one hundred years later, the Burnham (with an *h*) brothers established their successful joint business, which they eventually split between themselves. Murry built a two-story warehouse for his half—the mail-order business—near the intersection of U.S. 281 and RR 1431 where Broadway Showroom is now. Winston kept the retail store and the snakes.

Rhonda now lives with her husband in Harper, twenty miles west of Fredericksburg, though she visits Marble Falls often. Bill lives on a ranch in Round Mountain, about ten miles south of town.

Gary Roberson of Menard bought Burnham Brothers Sporting Goods in 1991. He moved the entire enterprise to Menard, where it remains the oldest game-calling business in the world, sans snakes.

PART VIII

HISTORY KEEPERS

Chapter 1

HISTORICAL COMMISSION LOOKS TO THE FUTURE IN HISTORY

The Burnet County Historical Commission has taken over the Old Burnet County Jail. Built in 1884, the stone two-story structure that housed prisoners for ninety-eight years was recently renovated to serve as a visitors' center and museum. For the first two years that the jail was open to the public, the only docent was the Burnet County tourism director. Now that the BCHC has moved into its first-ever brick-and-mortar facility, the jail is open to the public more often, with knowledgeable local historians giving tours.

The Burnet County Historical Commission is a branch of the county government. Members are appointed by the Burnet County commissioners in odd-numbered years. The BCHC applies for historical markers, lobbies for historic preservation and accepts museum items for local museum exhibits. Government entities must seek approval from the BCHC for certain road projects that could disturb hidden history.

The group's intervention preserved two historic bridges in the Joppa area: the Russell Fork Bridge on CR 272 and the North Fork San Gabriel Bridge on CR 200 east of Burnet. When the wooden and iron-truss bridges were due to be replaced by concrete, steel and asphalt, the federal government, which was providing most of the funding for the upgrade, stopped demolition plans for the aging structures after hearing from the commission.

"We still have the letter from the federal government saying these bridges are national treasures and cannot be destroyed," BCHC Chairman Rachel Bryson said. "To get the federal money, the bridges had to stay."

The Burnet County Historical Commission moved into the Old Burnet County Jail in 2024. *The Picayune Magazine.*

Bryson wrote a book about the bridges titled *North of Joppa, Volume I: The Iron Truss Bridges of Burnet County at Joppa.*

One of the biggest BCHC projects was researching, writing and publishing a two-volume tome, *Burnet County History*, both published in 1979. They also published *Cemetery Records, 1852–1953* and *Cemetery Records, 1953–1992.* The books became available online in 2024 and can be accessed on the hermanbrownlibrary.org website in the genealogy section. They are also available on the Falls on the Colorado Museum website at fallsmuseum.org. Click on "Learn" in the nav bar, then Resources and Links in the dropdown menu.

The commission plans to embark on a third Burnet County history volume soon. Author and historian Darrell Debo, who died in 2019, took on the job of compiling and editing the first two volumes for $100 a month. A host of volunteers worked with him.

"There were well over one hundred people who gathered, researched, interviewed and wrote an unbelievable amount of information that was submitted to Darrell," Bryson said of the first two volumes. "They contributed their research and stories without pay. Now it is forty-four years later and time to write volume three."

Volume three will upgrade family histories from 1900 to 1950, picking up where volume two left off in 1899. As before, families established in the county between those dates will write their own stories and submit them to be edited and included in volume three. The first volume contains the histories of businesses, churches and other organizations. The second volume lists families.

Together, at more than 350 pages each, the meticulously indexed books took ten years to complete. The money to publish came from the Burnet County commissioners, who were persuaded by Bryson's mother, Estelle Bryson, chairman of the historical commission for twenty years, and Willie Mae Price, then the head librarian at the Herman Brown Free Library in Burnet.

The commission is continuing to grow and regroup after the 2020 pandemic. The 2024 roster lists seventeen members compared to the thirty-four approved by commissioners in 2017. It has had as many as sixty-plus members in the past. In the coming years, it hopes to return to those glory days. Eight new members were inducted in January 2025.

"The pandemic hit us pretty hard," Bryson said. "Considering how fast this region is growing now, we are looking for people interested in learning about their new area to join us. We open our arms to anybody who can help us."

One of those new people is Amanda Seim, who moved with her husband to Burnet in 2021 and started a family. Seim has a master's degree in public history and worked as a program coordinator at the Compass Inn Museum outside Pittsburgh. She joined the Falls on the Colorado Museum Board of Directors and was chairman in 2024. She is also the genealogy librarian at the Herman Brown Free Library, which has an extensive archives and genealogy section.

Also new as of 2025 are Michael and Nichole Ritchie, two young history buffs who spend their free time cleaning tombstones and searching for lost markers. They discovered two missing Texas Centennial Markers, one in Burnet County and one in Llano County.

More than 1,100 markers commemorating the 100th birthday of the state of Texas were erected statewide by the Texas Historical Commission in 1936. Burnet County received two, both on U.S. 281, one at the Granite Mountain overlook south of Lake Marble Falls and one north of the city of

Burnet near the Lampasas County line. Both were missing until the Marble Falls marker was found at the bottom of a hill, where the Ritchies believe it was pushed by road crews widening the highway. The bronze plaques were long gone. The north Burnet marker has yet to turn up.

The marker found south of Marble Falls has been restored and placed on the Burnet Courthouse lawn, a process that included the Burnet County Historical Commission and the Burnet County commissioners. Nichole, a teacher, enlisted her Llano Middle School history class to help with the extensive bureaucratic process to restore the Llano marker and have it moved. That process was still underway in late 2024. The markers weigh about five thousand pounds each.

"The reason why we do it is to preserve [history]," Nichole told *The Picayune Magazine* in June 2022. "We find that very important because, you know, some guy just knocked this [Marble Falls marker] off the mountain as though it didn't matter. It will be nice to bring this in—even just for tourists—to show what Burnet County is about."

The Ritchies are now an integral part of the Stringtown Cemetery restoration, another important BCHC project.

"It's preserving something that was put there for a reason in the past," Michael told *The Picayune*. "And you're showing that one person, two people, can make a difference."

The BCHC has certainly made a difference in preserving history in its home county, especially with its growing slate of dedicated members. It facilitated moving an old iron-truss bridge due for demolition from private land to Johnson Park in Marble Falls.

At the behest of the Texas Historical Commission, BCHC began an inventory of the county's approximately eighty-eight historical markers in 2024, including those on each of the Joppa bridges, the Burnet County Courthouse, the Old Burnet County Jail and Dead Man's Hole. The most recent marker, for Buchanan Dam, has been approved and should be dedicated sometime in 2025.

Also, in 2024, the BCHC took over the Burnet County Jail and recovered a "lost" historical marker for the Conrad Fuchs House in Horseshoe Bay. The only known marker burned in a fire in February, but the THC found a match while renovating their Austin headquarters, tucked behind a bookcase. Until furniture was moved, no one knew a second marker existed. When Bryson was notified of the find, she immediately said, "That marker belongs back in Burnet County." Working with Falls on the Colorado Museum, BCHC negotiated a loan of the marker to the museum. It will be turned over when the museum completes its second-floor renovations.

"It is not our policy to do duplicate markers," THC Historical Marker Program historian Alicia Costello said. "It appears this marker was created as a sample marker to take to trade shows and various other events to promote the markers when the program first started. We're not quite sure which is the original and which is the replica."

The Conrad Fuchs House marker was one of the first granted by the newly formed Texas Historical Commission in 1974.

Another marker has been approved for 2025. THC awarded the Burnet commission a grant for an Untold History marker and renovation of Stringtown Cemetery, the only known all-Black cemetery in the county.

"It's important to keep history alive, to let people know how the places they live became what they are today," historian Seim said. "History fosters pride of place. With so much controversy during this time, one of the few things we can agree on is that we love where we live."

Chapter 2

HISTORY UNDERFOOT

To step onto the property of any of the three main history museums in the Highland Lakes is to step onto and into their biggest, most significant artifacts.

The Falls on the Colorado Museum in Marble Falls resides in a 133-year-old granite school building that began as a university in 1891. The Marble Falls Independent School District took it over in 1908, and one of its four elementary campuses now surrounds it. The two-story building housed classrooms until 1987 and MFISD administration offices until 2009. It has been home to the museum since 2010. In 2024, the school district granted $250,000 to renovate the second floor of the building for exhibits. The second floor had been deemed unsafe since the administration moved out.

Fort Croghan Museum and Grounds sits on the actual site of the fort, which was established in 1849 as one of four U.S. military outposts on the western frontier. Most of the historic buildings now on the property were moved to the site, but two are original to the location, including the cabin of the adjutant of the Second Dragoons of the Eighth Infantry U.S. (mounted).

The Llano County Historical Museum occupies the former Bruhl's Drugstore. The museum maintains the original soda fountain with leather stools and a marble bar. The 123-year-old building overlooks the Llano River and the Roy Inks Bridge, linking the northern half of the city of Llano to the south. The A.H. Bruhl family gave it to the Llano County Historical Society, which operates the museum, in 1965.

Each museum presents a unique and hyperlocal take on how Texas was shaped from its origins as part of Mexico through its independence as a nation and, finally, as the twenty-eighth state in the Union. Their very presence tells a story but wait until you step inside.

The Falls on the Colorado Museum

In Marble Falls, the tour of local history begins at the front door with a life-size replica of the inner workings of a corn and flour mill built by Lymon Wight and twenty Mormon families who settled near Marble Falls in 1851. Wight's group broke away from the Church of Jesus Christ of Latter-day Saints when founder Joseph Smith died, and Brigham Young took over. Those settlers eventually moved on from Marble Falls but left behind a Mormon cemetery, now on private land but still visited by descendants.

A few more steps inside and you'll find the answer to the question most museum visitors ask: why is the town named Marble Falls? A panoramic

A metal sculpture of General Adam R. Johnson in front of the Falls on the Colorado Museum in Marble Falls. *Suzanne Freeman.*

photo of the original falls shows the power that enticed Confederate General Adam R. Johnson to build a mill along the banks of the Colorado River. Blinded in battle in the Civil War, Johnson laid out city streets on a grid of letters and numbers based on his memory of surveying the land before the war. He was instrumental in the successful lobbying effort to bring a railroad to town in exchange for granite to build the Texas Capitol.

Farther down the main hall, the Granite Mountain exhibit features a ball and chain used to secure the convict labor shipped in to mine the capitol's building materials. The site remains an active quarry within the city limits.

Other highlights include a replica kitchen and bedroom from the late nineteenth and early twentieth centuries; the town room documenting historical leaders and businesses in the city's pre– and post–world war years; the education room, with its tribute to Marble Falls students; and space for traveling exhibits.

Dresses worn by Mayor Ophelia "Birdie" Harwood, who was elected when women did not have the right to vote, are also on display.

An entire room is dedicated to the seven-hundred-year-old bones of a bison uncovered by an amateur fossil hunter on the banks of South Rocky Creek in northeast Burnet County, along with Native American artifacts.

A book-filled room is perfect for digging through the museum's extensive archives. You can take a piece of history home by purchasing a book from the museum's collection, including those written by local historians.

The museum is expected to open its second floor to new exhibits sometime in 2025.

The Falls on the Colorado Museum at 2001 Broadway in Marble Falls is open from 10:00 a.m. to 2:00 p.m. Monday through Saturday. Admission is free; donations are appreciated. For more information, visit fallsmuseum.org, email focmuseum@gmail.com or call 830-798-2157.

Fort Croghan Museum and Grounds

Gravel pathways lead through a wooded area filled with cabins, farm implements and wildlife. Through each cabin door, visitors peer into Burnet County's pioneer past circa the mid-1850s when Fort Croghan, home to the U.S. Army Second Dragoon Regiment, was built to protect white settlers.

Inside the museum at Fort Croghan Museum and Grounds in Burnet. *Suzanne Freeman.*

The buildings include two original to the site: the army adjutant's office and a lookout that once sat atop Post Mountain at the edge of the thirty-eight-acre property.

Other cabins, which are all furnished and equipped as they would have been when first built, include the Logan Vandeveer cabin that once stood where the town's Dairy Queen on U.S. 281 is now, an old schoolhouse, a stagecoach stop converted into a post office and a working blacksmith shop. All were disassembled and rebuilt on the Fort Croghan grounds.

The blacksmith shop and a covered work area come alive with reenactors twice a year: the second weekend of October for Fort Croghan Day and the second Saturday of December for Christmas at Old Fort Croghan. Dressed in period costumes, volunteers weave baskets, grind cornmeal, braid rope, sew quilts, churn butter and hammer out horseshoes. They even wash clothes the pioneer way and hold lessons in the schoolroom.

Inside the museum, history moves back and forth and in between. While the grounds mainly depict life when the area was first settled, the air-conditioned museum contains exhibits on ancient times through the early 1900s.

The oldest items on display are original Native American headdresses and flint tools and weapons. The honor of next oldest belongs to a shawl from the Battle of San Jacinto, where Texas won its independence from Mexico, and a cannonball from the Battle of Goliad, another critical battle in the Texas Revolution.

The museum also has a World War I ambulance and the area's first fire engine.

Its growing collection keeps displays constantly changing as members of the Burnet County Heritage Society squeeze in donations in a meaningful, curated way.

Fort Croghan Museum and Grounds at 703 Buchanan Drive (Texas 29) in Burnet is open from 10:00 a.m. to 4:00 p.m. Thursday, Friday and Saturday, April 6–October 14, which is Fort Croghan Day. Christmas at Old Fort Croghan is the second Saturday in December. Admission is free; donations are appreciated. For more information, visit fortcroghan.com, email info@fortcroghan.com or call 512-756-8281.

LLANO COUNTY HISTORICAL MUSEUM

Whether you walk in the front door from the parking lot (which has only a few parking spots) or the back door (which has plenty of newly paved spaces), you step into the story of Llano County, from its covered wagon to its rock display.

The Llano County Historical Society has curated the museum's impressive collection around the industries and interests that built the area, beginning with the earliest white settlers in Castell and Bluffton.

On the shores of the Llano River, Castell still thrives as a tourism destination, while Bluffton, with its once-busy salt mines, lies on the bottom of Lake Buchanan. Its remains surface during droughts when the water level of Lake Buchanan, one of two reservoirs in the Highland Lakes chain, drops.

Minerals such as gold, iron and gadolinite—a mineral sought by Thomas Edison for use in his early experiments with lightbulbs—brought in people looking to strike it rich. Among the speculators was N.J. Badu, who built First National Bank, now the Badu House, in 1891. When mining didn't pan out, the area turned to ranching, agriculture and the railroad, which initially laid tracks to haul iron. The rails were soon moving cattle instead.

The original soda fountain at Bruhl's Drugstore, which opened in Llano in 1900, is still part of the building that now houses the Llano County Historical Museum. *Suzanne Freeman.*

A huge painting by local Western artist Jack Moss depicts the Battle of Packsaddle Mountain, the last known violent clash between white settlers and Native Americans in the area. The fight took place on August 5, 1873, and included several members of the Moss family, although not Jack's Moss family. Artist Moss organized a real-life reenactment of the scene at the location with descendants of the ranching Mosses, who were early Llano County founders. They still live on ranchlands that have been in the family for over a century.

In the lower right-hand corner of the battle painting, gun drawn, is an easily recognizable Jerry Don Moss, Llano County commissioner of Precinct 4, which includes the city of Llano and the museum. The chaps he wore for the reenactment belong to a Llano County Historical Society member whose father worked as a ranch hand for the Moss family for more than fifty years. Those same chaps hang on an adjacent wall in the museum.

Sitting front and center of the main museum room is a 1919 Studebaker Wagon purchased from the sale proceeds of a bale of cotton. If you come in the front door, it's the first thing you see as you walk by a marble-topped soda fountain to get there. The fountain was part of Bruhl's Drugstore, opened by German immigrant Louis Bruhl in 1900. The drugstore is now the museum's home.

The Llano County Historical Museum at 310 Bessemer Avenue (Texas 16) in Llano is open from 10:00 a.m. to 4:00 p.m. Wednesday through Saturday and at other times by appointment. Admission is five dollars for adults and three dollars for students and seniors. Ages five and younger and museum members get in free. For more information, visit llanomuseum.org or call 325-247-3026.

Chapter 3
HISTORY IN THE WORKS

A new museum is in the works in Marble Falls. St. Frederick Baptist Church began raising money in 2022 through grant applications, barbecues, bake sales and even staffing a fireworks stand for a Black history museum next door to their church at 301 Avenue N in Marble Falls. The pay-as-they-go effort has resulted in a roofed building with electricity, plumbing, windows and doors but, as of December 2024, no interior finish or air conditioning.

"We can do it bit by bit as we get the money," said Bessie Jackson, museum committee chair. "That way, we won't have any notes on the building."

For the Highland Lakes community, the Black history museum will be a modern-day education tool, Jackson said. She works closely with the Falls on the Colorado Museum and the Burnet County Historical Commission to collect artifacts, photos and documents and apply for grants.

"'Open the windows of heaven; I will pour you out a blessing,'" said Jackson, quoting Malachi 3:10 from the Old Testament of the Bible. "The more we give, the more comes in. As soon as we get down to nothing, God comes in."

That has certainly proven true when it comes to volunteers like Rueben Ortiz and his crew from Ortiz Concrete Co., who poured the slab.

"I wanted to find a place to give my time, and when I met Reverend [George] Perry, I knew what I wanted to do," Ortiz said. Perry is the minister of St. Frederick.

Reverend George Perry and Black History Museum Chairwoman Bessie Jackson of St. Frederick Baptist Church in Marble Falls, with some of the many items planned for exhibits. *Suzanne Freeman.*

The slab Ortiz poured proved an inspiration to Cecil Jackson (no relation) of Cecil Jackson Construction in Marble Falls.

"I kept driving by that slab and seeing it just sitting there, and then I heard Bessie on KBEY radio talking about how they needed volunteers, and that was it," Caleb Jackson said. "The Lord called me to help. It would have eaten me up if I hadn't done it."

KBEY 103.9 FM Radio Picayune is a local station that often features on-air interviews about local causes and events. Bessie Jackson is a frequent airwaves flyer.

A forty-plus-year resident of the Highland Lakes, Bessie Jackson served on the Marble Falls school district board and the Granite Shoals City Council. She worked at the pharmacy in H-E-B and for Lakeland Mall, a grocery and department store where H-E-B now stands in Marble Falls. She successfully fought to get her daughter, an A student, on the Marble Falls High School drill team.

The church has already collected quite a few artifacts and archives for the museum, much of which can be seen in the fellowship hall across the parking lot from the under-construction museum. The displays change frequently as new items are donated, and Jackson refocuses wall hangings on different historical figures or locals who have achieved success.

"I'm working on Harriet Tubman now and what she went through," Jackson said. "I want to use that to bring it home to people, like Mya [Berkman], who are successful despite hardships. I mean, if it had not been for Harriet Tubman, we would not have the opportunities to do what we are doing today."

Berkman has bachelor's and master's degrees in accounting from Liberty University in Lynchburg, Virginia, and is working on a master of business administration. She plays center for the Liberty Flames women's basketball team. Her list of accolades, both on and off the court, is too long for these pages. Photos in her St. Frederick's display include one of her with U.S. Supreme Court Justice Clarence Thomas and another of her and her teammates painted into the *Bigger Than Life* mural at Liberty University.

For the Tubman display, Jackson plans to showcase a quilt made by a group of women at Trinity Episcopal Church in Marble Falls. The quilt features some of the symbols believed to have been used as code by escaped slaves on the Underground Railroad, a series of secret routes slaves took to freedom. They looked for symbols on quilts, in the dirt or on buildings that led them north or helped them find safe places for food and rest.

Tubman was a station master on the Underground Railroad. She helped escaping slaves find sustenance and sanctuary and is closely linked to the freedom quilts in history.

Symbols used included a wrench quilt block indicating it was time to prepare the tools needed for escape; a wagon wheel meaning load up and go; a bear's paw advising people to use a mountain trail; and a log cabin assuring freedom seekers that a home was a safe place for food or rest. The symbols, derived from African art, communicated necessary information to people who could not read or write and did not know U.S. geography.

"A lot of people don't understand the logistics of the freedom quilts," Jackson said. "Not only did the quilts serve as warmth, they were used as a code system to communicate."

Along with highlighting national figures in Black history, the museum will spotlight Black community members who graduated from Marble Falls High School and have gone on to make a difference in the world, like Berkman and Jackson's daughter Becky Smith Davis of Atlanta.

"She's the owner of a company called the Bosspreneur Business Circle," Jackson said of her daughter. "She was featured in *Essence* magazine in their November/December issue [2020]. She's been on a lot of magazine covers."

Other examples are Marquita Pride, who was appointed by Governor Greg Abbott to the State Board of Dental Examiners in 2021; Charles Washington, who retired after twenty years in the U.S. Marine Corps; and Marble Falls High School track star Ann Foster, who was inducted into the Abilene Christian University Sports Hall of Fame.

And there are more.

"They don't teach that in schools," Jackson said. "Some of these kids come from horrible backgrounds, but they did not use that as an excuse. They overcame that and are successful."

The ultimate hope is that highlighting successful locals will inspire others to work harder.

"If we can get some knowledge out there for our kids to see and be inspired, then they can say, 'I need to do better, I'm somebody,'" Jackson said. "This is knowledge-based. That's how it helps. Teach me, teach me, teach me. Teach me there is hope. If you don't know you can do better, then you are not going to do any better."

Once completed, the museum will be open for tours and school field trips.

"If we don't get but one to get out of the rut, I think it'd be worth it all," she said. "If you take away the stigma that you're not going to be anything, then you have equal opportunity."

The St. Frederick Black History Museum is designed to highlight and encourage that opportunity.

"If I can help somebody before I pass along then my living won't be in vain," Jackson said. "I want everybody to be the best they can be."

Progress on the building comes in waves. After each major piece of the puzzle is completed, the project appears stalled while fundraisers and grant applications continue. None of that worries Reverend Perry, who began a final push in December 2024 with hopes of opening the doors in 2025.

"When the Lord says it's time to finish, it's time to finish," Perry said.

BIBLIOGRAPHY

Books

Banks, Herbert C., II, ed. *Daughters of the Republic of Texas: Patriots Ancestor Album*. Turner Publishing, 2001.

Bryson, Rachel. *North of Joppa*. Vol. 1, *The Iron Truss Bridges of Burnet County at Joppa*. Burnet County Historical Commission, 2016.

Caro, Robert. *Path to Power*. Vintage, 1990.

Daniel, Lewis E. *Types of Successful Men of Texas*. E. Von Boeckmann, 1890.

Debo, Darrell. *Burnet County History*. Vol. 1. Eakin Press, 1979.

————. *Burnet County History*. Vol. 2. Eakin Press, 1979.

Dixon, Sam Houston, and Louis Wiltz Kemp. *The Heroes of San Jacinto*. Anson Jones Press, 1932.

Fehrnebach, T.R. *Comanches: The Destruction of a People*. Replica Books, 1974.

Jorden, James R. *A History of the Conrad L. Fuchs Family and the Fuchs House of Burnet County*, Texas. Self-published, 2020.

Knapik, Jane, and Amanda Rose. *Images of America: Marble Falls*. Arcadia Publishing, 2013.

Moursund, John Stribling. *Blanco County History*. Nortex Press, 1979.

Polk, Stella Gipson. *The Mason County War*. Eakin Press, rev. 1980.

Shelby, Maurice C. *The Lake Victor Story*. Second printing, Lake Victor, TX: Maurice Shelby, 1972.

Smithwick, Noah. *The Evolution of a State: Recollections of Old Texas Days*. Gammel Book Company, 1900.

Newspaper and Magazine Articles

Baughman, J.L. "The Mountain Where Texas Skyscrapers Were Born." *Houston Chronicle Rotogravure Magazine*, August 16, 1953.

Bryson, Rachel. "Stringtown Became post–Civil War Enclave for Burnet County's African-Americans." *Picayune*, March 2007.

Burnham, W.L. "Vivid Recollections of 80 Years in Burnet County." *Burnet Bulletin*, June 30, 1938.

Carmack, George. "Granite Mountain Sturdy Texas Native." *San Antonio Express-News*, February 6, 1982.

Debo, Darrell. "Logan Vandeveer and Burnet." *Burnet County Bulletin*, May 16, 1974.

Gibbs, Alta Holland. "Four Grand Old Men—Our Trail Blazers." *Burnet Bulletin*, June 30, 1938.

Gray, L.R. "Letter to the Editor re: Dead Man's Hole." *Marble Falls Messenger*, October 24, 1939.

Gregg, Savanna. "Fuchs' House Survival Crucial to County's Preservation." *Highlander*, May 14, 2019.

Hanson, Susan. "Texas Granite Had a Role in Our History." *San Marcos Daily Record*, January 21, 1990.

Harwood, Ophelia "Birdie." "Why I Am Running for Mayor of Marble Falls." *Marble Falls Messenger*, March 15, 1917.

Martin, Nicholas. "A.B. McGill and the General Store." *TAMS Journal of the Token and Medal Society*, November–December 2013.

Meador, J.T. "How Deadman's Cave Got Its Name." *Texas Caver*, February 1965.

Mitchell, Anita. "Capitol Granite Donor Credited…Finally." *The Highlander*, August 15, 1985.

Posey, Mary Johnson. "Captive Beauty, Miss King Rescued in Bloody Indian Fight: Logan Van Deveer Was a Hero." *Hunter's Frontier Times Magazine*, June 1938.

———. "Sherrard's Cave in Burnet County." *Frontier Times Monthly*, April 1926.

———. "Terrific Indian Fight with Knives in a Cave Gave Logan Van Deveer, Austin's First Owner, His Beautiful Bride." *Austin American*, February 24, 1918.

Richter, Walter. "Disaster at Dead Man's Hole." *Frontier Times* 18, no. 6, March 1941.

Rigler, Frank C. "Logan Vandeveer's Early Texas Days, Parts I, II, and II." *Highlander*, April 1972

Russell, Karylon Hallmark. "The Legacy of Johnny Ringo." *Llano News*, October 19, 2011.

Warton, Mike. "Resurrection Well: Texas Speleological Survey." *Texas Caver*, August 1990.

Archives

Fort Croghan archives. Fort Croghan Grounds and Museum in Burnet.

Frank Dalton papers, 2.325/A157. Dolph Briscoe Center for American History. University of Texas at Austin.

Granite Mountain archives. Falls on the Colorado Museum in Marble Falls.

Granite School archives. Falls on the Colorado Museum in Marble Falls.

Thomas Ferguson. Johnny Ringo file. Fort Croghan Grounds and Museum.

Video

Cosmatos, George P., and Kevin Jarre, dirs. *Tombstone*. 1993.

Historical Narratives

Holmes, Nell Harwood, d. 2017. "A History of Dr. and Mrs. George Hill George Hill Harwood." Falls on the Colorado Museum, 1993.

House Resolution No. 340, 59th Legislative session, Kate Shuford Craddock, by Representative James Terrell "Terry" Townsend, Texas House of Representatives, April 14, 1965.

Pickle, J.J. "Jake." "Max Starcke—Builder of Central Texas." *Congressional Record, U.S. House of Representatives Minutes*, Bound Copy, 24860–861, July 20, 1972.

Weaver, Esther Richter, b. 11-9-1914, d. 11-8-1992. "History of the Conrad Fuchs Rock House." Undated typewritten narrative in the archives of Falls on the Colorado Museum, Marble Falls.

Zimmerman, June. Lucille S. Craddock, Ralph Smith. Handwritten letter, July 1989.

Zimmerman, Minnie Boutwell. "The Henry Flaugher Family Texas Experience 1848–1863." Typewritten narrative, January 2008.

Websites

Daltondatabank.org. "Frank Dalton: The 'Good Brother of the Gang.'" Researched, complied and edited by Rodney G. Dalton. www.daltondatabank.org/Chronicles/Frank_Dalton.htm.

Find a Grave. "Samuel Ely Holland." www.findagrave.com/memorial/22683870/samuel-ely-holland.

Fort Smith National Historic Site. "Frank Dalton: Deputy US Marshal." National Park Service. www.nps.gov/fosm/learn/historyculture/frank-dalton-deputy-us-marshal.htm.

Legislative Reference Library. "Samuel Ely Holland." lrl.texas.gov/legeleaders/members/memberdisplay.cfm?memberID=3808.

Lower Colorado River Authority. "LCRA Historical Timeline—1890s to Present." lcra.org/about/overview/history.

Officer Down Memorial Page. "Deputy U.S. Marshal Frank Dalton." www.odmp.org/officer/3769-deputy-us-marshal-frank-dalton.

Texas Hill Country. "The Bluebonnet House: The Story of the Iconic Hill Country House Parts 1–5." June 10, 2015. texashillcountry.com/bluebonnet-house-iconic.

About the Author

David Bean.

Suzanne Warwick Freeman is editor of *The Picayune Magazine* in Marble Falls. She has a bachelor's degree from the University of Texas at Austin and a master's degree from the Columbia Graduate School of Journalism in New York. She worked as an editor at Scholastic Inc. in New York for fourteen years before returning to her roots in Central Texas. While at Scholastic, she started the award-winning Scholastic Kids Press Corps, traveling nationwide to cover presidential politics, the Olympics and major entertainment and sporting events. She lives in Austin, Texas, with her teenage daughter and, when not reporting and writing, spends time with her four grandchildren.